The Spiritual Path to Prosperity…
The Truth about Money Revealed

Dawn Santoriello, CFP®

BookLocker

Saint Petersburg, Florida

Published by BookLocker.com, Inc., St. Petersburg, Florida.

Printed on acid-free paper.

BookLocker.com, Inc.
2021

First Edition

Disclaimer

This book has been written solely for informational and educational purposes. No content constitutes professional or individual-specific financial advice. While best efforts were employed when writing this book to include accurate, verifiable content, the author or anyone else who may have been involved in any way in the preparation of this book makes no representations or warranties of any kind and assumes no liabilities as related to the accuracy or completeness of the information presented.

The author and all parties involved in the preparation of this book shall not be held liable for any loss or damages caused or alleged to have been caused directly or indirectly by the information presented herein.

Every individual's financial situation is unique, and the information and strategies in this book speak to the book's audience in general and may not apply to your specific situation. You should always seek the services of a certified financial professional before attempting or implementing any of the strategies detailed in this book.

Advisory Services offered by Sowell Management.

This book is dedicated to my parents. Without the both of you, I wouldn't be the woman I am today. Thank you for adopting me and inspiring me to believe in myself and that I could achieve anything to which I set my mind.

Table of Contents

Acknowledgments

First and foremost, I want to thank God/Spirit/Love Energy/Universe. You have guided me through all my days, the light and the dark and made me the woman I am today. My life flows much easier when I listen to your divine guidance.

Thank you to my family. I love you guys.

To my spiritual teacher, Lynn Rene Macdonald, thank you for teaching me the prayer that has changed my life and the lives of countless others. I am so glad you are in my life. Thank you for all your love and support.

Thank you to my editor, Brigid Levi, for bringing the book to life.

Thank you to all the people at BookLocker.com for helping me get this published.

Thank you to Rick Williams who never gave up on me when I didn't return his calls. Your friendship and help with my business have been greatly appreciated.

Thank you to Don Blanton for teaching me the truth about how life insurance works.

Thank you, Steve Miller and Zack Shepard for teaching me the truth about how investments work.

Thank you to all the friends and colleagues I have made along my journey, including Lee Ann Dalgliesh, Jeff Ryan, Antoine Orr, Stephen Mathieu and many others. You all know who you are.

Thank you, Jim Barbee, for making sure I dotted my Is and crossed my Ts and kept me in compliance.

A special thank you to my Fem City family, especially Violette de Ayala. I love you all and appreciate you immensely. Violette, thanks for giving me a platform for my voice to be heard.

Introduction

My soul's calling is to show people the truth about money so they can have more abundance and peace of mind in reaching their goals. I love making a positive difference in their lives when it comes to showing them how money really works. Study after study shows people want help when it comes to their finances. But where are these people? Even with all my experience, my many articles and my YouTube show, my phone isn't ringing off the hook. There is so much confusing and conflicting information in our industry. Most financial planners won't work with you unless you have an account minimum balance of $500,000. But I don't have an account minimum.

As well as being a CERTIFIED FINANCIAL PLANNER™ (CFP®), I am also an Independent Advisor Representative (IAR), and in this role, I work for a Registered Investment Advisor (RIA). RIAs are registered investment advisory firms which provide financial planning, investment advisory, and wealth management services for clients in a fiduciary capacity. In the past, I have dealt with many frustrations in my industry, one of those being the high fees that my RIA charged for myself and my clients. Every time I would complain to my RIA about the fees being too high I was told, "No they are not. We just brought on an adviser whose clients were paying 3%, and he paid his company $650 a month. Dawn, you are the only one complaining about the fees. You have the option to lower your fee."

Yes, I could lower my fee, but as a result, I would have a lower payout percentage to me. But the RIA firm is still billing the client the same amount of money regardless of what I charge. How fair is that? I was also told that since we are governed by the SEC, our fees have to be "reasonable." Because the SEC is our governing body and we are fiduciaries, I considered that I might have been wrong. When I set out to do my own research, I found out I was not wrong. I've spoken with other

RIA firms, advisors, money managers, professors, and tax advisors. They all agreed with me. Any investment management fee over 2% is too high. So now I had this dilemma: how could I continue to bring new clients onto this platform when I now saw the truth? I couldn't. So, I asked to bring on a low-cost money manager and was told the RIA will look into it. They never did.

At that time, I also learned about the Efficient Market Hypothesis Theory (from another money management firm), which basically says no one can beat the market consistently over time. The models my RIA was using were actively managed, meaning trying to beat the market. This new firm was interested in my success and in helping my clients. That is a rarity in this industry. I was impressed with all they had to offer me and my clients. I was vetted and approved by that RIA but with conditions. Initially, I had to script my *Financial Fridays with Dawn!* YouTube show and run all my insurance contracts through them. Meaning, I couldn't keep my direct contracts and relationships I had with my insurance companies. This was an independent RIA firm. How independent is that if I have to give up control? Having a choice is the reason I became independent. Disheartened, I checked with other RIA firms and was told a similar story. If they didn't want my insurance contracts, I had to use their money manager. This is not true independence. As it turns out, this new RIA changed their minds when I signed with them. I was able to do my show and write insurance through any company of my choice — good companies, obviously.

If I had my own RIA I could have the freedom I am looking for, but there would be drawbacks, such as the amount of compliance and time it would take to set it up. And the resources that would be available to me might be limited based on the size of my firm at this time. I'd rather have that taken care of for me and focus on my clients and their needs. Who knows? Maybe this would work for me in the future. At that point, I trusted in Love Energy (God) that everything would happen exactly the way it was supposed to, and it did. I'll get to that in a minute.

Back to that RIA that was frustrating the hell out of me. They built Exchange Traded Funds (ETF) portfolios, which have a lower cost to the client, and the advisors also get paid a lot less. However, there is still a price disparity if the advisors charge a lower fee. The RIA should allow us to charge what we want and still have the same percentage payout. But the current model is flawed and benefits the RIA.

It's hard to continue down a path once you see the light and now know the truth. The last few months I was with that firm was very stressful for me. Every time I tried to better the situation for my clients and myself, I was confronted with the hypocrisy in our industry. As advisors, we are supposed to put our clients' needs ahead of our own, but the RIAs seem to put their needs ahead of the clients by telling their advisors what products they can use. Thanks to someone at the firm who believed as I did, they are moving in a better direction, but there is still more to go.

At least now I'm able to sleep at night knowing I am putting my clients' needs first and not overcharging them. I love and care about all my clients. I am so grateful to all of them who have stuck with me throughout my career. They know that I do my best and always look out for them. I enjoy the whole process of showing them a better way to reach their goals by becoming more efficient with their money and putting a holistic plan together for them. It is a great feeling when a client truly appreciates what I have done for them and to see them reach their financial goals.

I decided to write this book to share with people that everyone can have a prosperous, fulfilling life. *The Spiritual Path to Prosperity* has three components: prayer, a positive mindset (free of money blocks), and knowing how to manage your finances properly. Anything is possible when you are in alignment with God/Spirit/Love

Energy/Universe. I follow my inner guidance, and it has helped me. That guidance gave me the courage this year to combine spirituality and money, and I have created new programs to help so many people. It also led to the creation of this book.

Everything does work out at the right time. I am currently with the RIA firm that my new money manager introduced me to and things are going well. I am happy with the level of service and offerings that are available to help me grow and be the best planner I can be for my clients. The new firm has good values and puts their advisors and clients first. I'm happy I made the switch and can now focus on what matters most—helping my clients and other people who need me.

1. What Made Me Want to Be a Financial Planner

I was born in the Park Slope neighborhood of Brooklyn, New York in 1978. My family was poor, and my parents were addicted to drugs and alcohol. When I was two years old, my dad died of a drug overdose which was the story I was told. But just this year, I learned through a DNA test (23andme) that he wasn't my dad. But that's another story for another time. My mom was a drug addict and heavy drinker and not around much, so my grandmother was the one who raised my sister and me.

We were so poor that I had a black hole in my front tooth because we couldn't afford to go to the dentist. Thank God it was just a baby tooth. Even so, I have fond memories of my time with my grandmother. My favorite meal she made us—that I still eat to this day—is egg noodles and cottage cheese with salt and pepper. Most people's reaction to this is "Ugh, gross." Try it. It's delicious! She tried her best to give us healthy meals with what little money we had.

When our grandmother could no longer take care of us, my sister and I were in and out of foster homes. At one point, we lived with her biological dad. He didn't like me because I wasn't his, so he would beat me with his belt. I remember he even threw me in a dryer, but I don't remember if he turned it on. The foster homes we lived in weren't much better. One family made my sister and I eat in the kitchen while they sat together in the dining room. We also couldn't have anything to drink until we ate all our food.

Fortunately, my sister and I eventually ended up in a great foster home, and that family ended up adopting us. I was ten and remember that day well. The judge gave my sister and me these huge, swirly lollipops, and then we went to our favorite diner afterwards for breakfast.

I never wanted to be poor again, and I wanted to help other people gain financial security. Early on, I realized the importance of financial stability, especially after my adoptive family provided that for me. I wanted to become a financial planner to help people avoid the scary childhood I had.

Even as a child, entrepreneurship was in my blood. I took every opportunity I could to earn money. There was an apple tree and a chestnut tree in my backyard, and my dad would pay me and my four sisters ten cents a bag to pick them. I made sure I hustled and always filled the most bags. Sometimes, my dad took me to his office on Saturdays, and he paid me two dollars an hour to do some filing while he worked. When it snowed, I shoveled driveways. I saved my daily lunch money and made my own lunch to bring to school instead. When I was in high school, I sold Blow Pops that I bought from BJs. I would make about fifty dollars a week doing that. Then, some other kids decided to do it, and they got caught. I didn't know we weren't allowed to sell candy if it didn't benefit the school. So, I quit before I got caught, too. Through all this, I kept a little accounting journal and had subaccounts for car, house, and CDs (the music kind). I loved watching the accounts grow!

Before I found my love of finance, my first love was acting and modeling. Once I realized that was keeping me broke, I left the industry and got started in financial services. I never thought I could love anything else besides acting and modeling, but I was wrong. I only wish I found this career sooner than at age twenty-six.

You have to love this career because up to 90% of advisors fail within their first year. The rest are just scraping by unless they are lucky enough to land a wealthy client or have a senior partner to work alongside. I wasn't so lucky. I had to start from scratch.

2. The Early Days

Most people think that if you are in the financial services industry you make a lot of money. According to Glassdoor, the average salary is $28,000 to $115,000, though some people earn way more. If you can be as lean as possible, you can run your business for about $25,000 to $50,000 a year. That doesn't leave much left for everything else when you are starting out. What people don't realize when they get into this business is that everything you do costs money—from marketing, to compliance fees, E&O insurance, education, technology, office equipment, etc. Even if you work independently for another company, you are paying for this. When I started out, I paid over $800 a month just for a cubicle!

Early in my career, I remember not having enough money to get out of a parking garage. It was a cold January day, and there was a line of cars forming behind me. My credit card kept getting declined, and I didn't have any cash. In fact, I only had $200 to my name! I hit the buzzer to get a service person, and after five long minutes (and an ever-growing line), someone came out and opened the gate for me. It was so embarrassing! Little did I know I would later have my first six-figure year.

I got home that night and cried. With no new clients on the horizon, I didn't know what I was going to do. I was single in a field where two incomes are better than one, and I was in the middle of a housing remodel that was draining my finances. And I couldn't even pay to leave a parking garage!

The solution was to get a part time job where no one would recognize me until business picked up. God forbid a client saw me, revealing my lack of success (so far, at least). So, I did manual labor for my neighbor, who was also remodeling his house. For $10 an hour, I scraped paint off of walls and cabinets, dug in the dirt, and lifted heavy objects.

I couldn't put in many hours because I had to work my day job, so I tried bartending on the weekends. A successful, popular bar was out of the question because I might see someone I knew. Instead, I went to a seedy, local corner bar where the owner had allegedly raped someone in the back room. I made sure a friend of mine was with me at closing time so I wasn't alone. Compared to what bartenders at successful bars brought in, I hardly made any money. After dealing with drunk, perverted men for about two and a half months, my soul just couldn't take it anymore, so I quit.

I was getting a small sale here and there but nothing substantial. To help pay for the housing remodel, I decided to take out a personal loan and borrowed a few bucks from my Dad, which I didn't want to do because of my pride. I wanted to be able to say that I was the only one in my family that didn't ask my dad for money.

At the time, I thought this shouldn't be my life. I was a financial planner. I knew how to create wealth and grow money. I'd helped my clients create more money than they thought was possible, but for some reason, I couldn't do it for myself. I was blocked. I was spiritually blocked around money, and all of my analytical skills couldn't save me.

So, how did I get unblocked? It started with a prayer and a vision board. The prayer helped me clear my money blocks, open the doors to wealth, and change my finances in a way I didn't think was possible.

So, I've been where most of you have been. Some of you are just starting out in your careers and maybe some of you left the corporate world to pursue your dream of owning a business. It's not easy starting a business from scratch, but I was up for the challenge. I have done it three times in three different locations. I even moved to a different state. In one area, I only knew my two brothers and my boyfriend, none of whom became clients right away.

I didn't know it at the time, but things were about to change in a big way for me. A guy from a marketing company named Rick had been bugging me for almost four months, and I thought he was trying to sell me newsletters, so I just ignored him. One day—I'm not sure why—I decided to take his call. He explained that he wasn't trying to sell me newsletters but that he helped advisors with their marketing, case design, and generating leads. And he wanted to help me, too. I wished I'd answer his call sooner! Being stubborn isn't good all the time. Because of the cost of his program, I didn't sign up for it, but instead, Rick and I spoke every now and then for the next couple of months.

One day, he called me to tell me about a conference I should attend where I would learn more about this one insurance company and sales ideas for their products. Immediately, I turned it down because I assumed this would cost a lot of money. When he said his marketing company would cover the full cost including airfare, I was in. The conference was to take place a month or two later.

As luck would have it, shortly after that phone call, I sideswiped my car with another car driving down my block. (I'm not good with spatial awareness.) The seven-year-old car had about 140,000 miles on it, but since it was in good condition prior to the accident, I had dropped my collision coverage. I was driving around with the driver's side all scraped up and a dent in my mirror, and the following week, I had to go meet a client at his country club. I tried to hide the damage by parking in the back lot in what I thought was a secluded spot. That didn't work. My client came in and said, "Dawn, what happened to your car?"

After another embarrassing moment, I went home and prayed that my car would be totaled. What happened next was an absolute miracle. The next morning in the middle of my yoga class, a guy walked in and asked if anyone had a white car parked out front. It was mine. He suggested I go take a look at it, and when I walked out, I saw that my car was literally pushed up on the sidewalk against a pole. The back tire was messed up, and now the driver's side had more than just a dent in the mirror; the entire door was dented! Luckily, I was in yoga class so I was calm and didn't immediately freak out. At first, I thought, "How in the world did this just happen?" But then I realized, "OMG my prayer was just answered!" I was in shock.

I don't remember the exact details, but allegedly, it was the father's car and the son used it all the time, or it was the son's car and the insurance only covered him. But in any case, the son and his girlfriend had a fight, and she took off in the car, hitting my car and two others along the way. My car took the worst of it.

After class, my friend took me to look at some Hondas, and that's when reality set in. I couldn't afford to get a new car. What was I going to do? Luckily, I didn't have to make a decision right away because the next day, I flew out to the conference that Rick had planned for me.

It was amazing! I learned a strategy that helped a lot of my clients. Unfortunately, it didn't work for all my clients. What works for someone might not work for others. On the bright side, this one little idea made me $80,000 in one month! Needless to say, I had my best year ever, earning over six figures!

When I returned from the conference, though, I still had to deal with my car. The owner of the other vehicle tried to say his son didn't have permission to use the car blah blah blah. When the insurance adjuster called me, I told her how it was in Scranton. The car owner was a well-know, successful businessman in the area. The men in Scranton thought they were so powerful and above the law, and they were always trying to pull one over on others, especially women. I told her what he was doing was wrong and unjust. He should do the right thing and not try to escape his obligation to the insurance company. After a week, my car was totaled, and I received a check for over $7,000—more than what I was expecting!

It gets better.

My friend from yoga class suggested we check out the Acura's even though they were out of my price range. Well, it turned out I got a fully loaded leftover model for less than I would have paid for the Honda! I learned many lessons that year, including having faith that everything will work out in your favor even if it may not seem that way at the time.

I got into this business because I had a Bachelor's degree in finance. I loved helping people, and my acting and modeling career didn't work out. Today, I can't imagine doing anything else. I am so passionate about what I get to do every day, and I am always learning something new to help my clients. I create programs that help my clients reach their personal and professional goals as well as motivate them to go and achieve their dreams. I get to choose the clients I want to work with, and best of all, I can work anywhere is the world with my laptop and an internet connection.

If you are passionate about something, go for it whole-heartedly, and you will reach your goals. Even if you don't reach the exact goal you envisioned, you will be in a better place than you are today. There will be the naysayers, but don't let them deter you.

When I decided to enter the insurance field, I told my former supervisor, and she tried to talk me out of it. She said her husband was very smart, and he couldn't make it. In fact, most people don't make it in this field. That wasn't going to be me.

Even my dad told me to get a job that paid a salary instead of the commission-only job I was first offered. He was just trying to protect his daughter like dads do. But being the stubborn daughter I am, I ignored this advice and accepted the job offer. He eventually came around when I began my career at MetLife, and I remember him telling me, "Dawn, now don't try to take over the company in six months." I never even thought of owning my own business, and sixteen years later here I am, founder of DS Financial Strategies.

My biggest takeaways from that first six-figure year are this: Do whatever it takes to make your dreams come true even if you have to take on a side hustle; don't be close minded; and finally, don't drop your collision insurance!

3. How I Work With the Law of Attraction

I met my friend and spiritual teacher Lynn Rene MacDonald a few years ago. I was already on my spiritual journey for some time when I ran into her at a mall. At the time, I was going through a rough period in life as we all do and had prayed the night before to have God send me someone to help me. I woke up that morning and felt the need to go to the mall. I didn't want to go, but when your intuition tells you to do something, you listen.

It turned out there was a health fair going on. I met some really interesting people, one being Lynn. As I approached her, I could tell she was a high-vibing intuitive, and she had great energy. I realized, then, that she was the answer to my prayer.

Since our meeting at the mall, she has taught me a prayer that has changed my life and has caused miracles to happen for me! She taught me how to create my life and continually helps me clear all my blocks: emotional, financial, spiritual—you name it! Within two years of meeting her, I manifested my dream car and my dream boyfriend at that time!

One powerful way this prayer worked for me was when I was moving into a gorgeous new apartment. I ordered a couch, but it was going to be delivered before my move in time, and the apartment complex wouldn't give me the keys the night before. So, I did the prayer, and when the delivery truck arrived, we found a side door open in the garage at the exact time someone was walking out of the elevator. We were able to get in the door that would have been locked, and my couch was delivered all the way to my apartment door.

An important thing about the prayer is that once you say it, you have to let it go. Don't dwell on it and try to figure out how it's going to happen. Just let it go. Letting go is an extremely important part of the process. If you don't let it go, you remain stuck in "wanting" something so you will manifest more "wanting."

This prayer can be important when it comes to finances. You know you want more money, and you have cleared the external blocks that you are aware of, but your finances still aren't quite right, so you call upon Spirit to clear any subconscious blocks. This solves the problem of being guided by lack and blocking abundance! Some blocks may not clear up instantly, so it's important to continue clearing and praying.

If we are only relying on ourselves, when things become difficult, we feel stuck and lost.

We may feel frustrated, panic, and make mistakes when it comes to our money because we want a certain outcome, and we think we know the best way to get it. Money will start to control our life if we block its natural flow by worrying about it so much. It will become all we think about.

How can we solve this? With a little help from Spirit and the Law of Attraction. The Law of Attraction states that positive thoughts create positive circumstances and negative thoughts create negative circumstances. By saying the prayer I'm about to share with you in times of unease, stress, or anxiety about money, you will free yourself from worry because you let your Higher Power handle it for you. You will be calmer and more receptive to new ideas and inspirations that Spirit is trying to send you to help your finances. Finally, you will have financial peace of mind and manifest abundance!

Here is the prayer:

"Thank you God for this for me (insert what you want in the present tense) in the best way for me and all or something better! And thank you God for that for me. Thank you God for clearing, changing, and healing anything in my soul or anything I say, do, or create that prevents this prayer from being answered. Let me be free from it now, please. And thank you God for that for me."

Another version of the prayer that I have been having even more success with is this one:

1. Ask Love to speak through me.
2. Ask Love to handle it.
3. Ask Love to clear any blocks that are keeping my prayers from being answered.
4. Ask Love to be happy no matter what happens.
5. Thank you God for that for me.

"Love, speak through me now and handle (insert whatever you are seeking). Love, clear; heal; and change anything that would prevent this prayer from being answered. Love, let me be happy no matter what, and thank you God for that for me."

Lynn likes to remind me that everything happens in God's time, not my time. In order to manifest your dreams, you also must be in your heart space. As you progress along in your journey, things change as you change, but everything you need to grow is given to you at the right time. Sometimes, you have to experience certain circumstances in order to understand what you do or don't want in your life.

There you have it. I can't wait to hear about your successes with this powerful prayer. After attending one of my webinars, "Releasing the 5 Biggest Money Blocks Holding You Back," a friend of mine said this prayer, and four days later she received a $30,000 ghost writing job! How awesome is that? If it can work for my friend, it can work for you, too!

4. What I Do and Why I Do It

What makes me qualified to give financial advice? Besides walking the walk from poverty to six figures, I went to Adelphi University and received my B.S. in Finance. When I decided to go into the financial services industry, I also had to pass a series of tests: Life, Accident, Health, Series 63, and 65. I actually quit my job and moved to Scranton the Friday before I took my first test. If I didn't pass the test that Monday, I would be unemployed for 30 days. I took a leap of faith and luckily it worked out because I passed the test. My first year in the business, I also earned my first designation, Life Underwriter Training Council Fellow or LUTCF. This consisted of passing five classes from the American College.

Years later I wanted to take my practice to the next level, so I enrolled in the CERTIFIED FINANCIAL PLANNER™ (CFP®) program. This was no easy task. I took the self-study route. I had to take six classes including tax, insurance, financial planning, retirement planning, investments and estate planning. I also had to present a financial plan to a professor who was assigned to me. I needed someone who was already a CFP® to write a recommendation for me, and I needed to have at least three years of planning experience.

After each course I had to go to an exam center and pass a final exam before I could move on to the next course. I had passed each exam on my first try. When I enrolled in the investments class, however, I psyched myself out. The person enrolling me said he dropped out of this class because it was so difficult. I ended up quitting halfway through because it did become difficult, and I was afraid I would fail the exam. So, I took a three-year break.

But I'm not a quitter. I wanted to finish what I started, so I completed my last two courses in one year. I also did my financial plan (they call it the Capstone class) without a break in between and signed up for the review class for the CFP® exam, which I was scheduled to take later that year. I was concerned because the exam covers all six classes, and I had a big gap in my studies. But thanks to Brett Danko's review class, I am proud to say I passed my CFP® exam on my first try. The questions are tricky, so you really have to know your stuff inside and out. My heart was pounding when I hit "enter" to see my results. Seeing PASSED made me so happy! I couldn't believe it. I was shaking. Only 62% pass on their first try. That was the hardest test I have ever taken in my life!

As a CFP®, it is my mission to teach people the truth of how money really works so they can reach their financial goals with peace of mind. I also want to inspire economic confidence within everyone.

Let's face it. Money is a confusing topic for many people. There is a lot of stress and anxiety around money, which sometimes leaves people feeling overwhelmed. I am passionate about educating people on how to invest for the long-term. My mission in life is to help people by showing them the truth about money and cut through all the noise that is out there when it comes to growing your money for the long haul.

I love helping people manage their money and reaching their goals by providing them with information that is clear and easy to digest. The big problem I see is that so many people struggle to find the clarity and confidence they need to take action when it comes to their money. Some may lack confidence in their knowledge. Some are overwhelmed by information and decisions. Others are too busy to deal with handling their money and want to know they are using proven real-world investment strategies.

When you let go of fear and change your beliefs about money, your clarity and confidence will change, too. Once you clear your money blocks, you can make the best use of proven real-world investment strategies to make the most of the money you already have. Having a written financial plan and someone like me to help you avoid costly mistakes will improve your current and future financial situation.

In order to fulfill our destinies, we need to get our financial house in order and understand how money works. I've written this book to help you do just that. This book will help you quickly remove spiritual blocks around money so you can step into a life without debt, retire sooner than you thought you could, and accumulate wealth so you can achieve your dreams. I'll teach you how to grow your money without complicated strategies or big sacrifices in your day-to-day life. If you want your money to work harder so you don't have to, keep reading!

5. Releasing the Five Biggest Money Blocks That Are Holding You Back

Before we get into the different financial products and strategies used to accumulate wealth, it's important that we clear any money blocks that are keeping us stuck in the same situation. Without clearing these blocks, it doesn't matter if you know how money works because you won't be able to hold onto it long enough to use the strategies. Look at me for example. I was making my clients money, and they were doing well. But I didn't know I had subconscious blocks around money that were holding me back from reaching my goals. Once I cleared them, money and business opportunities started flowing in unexpected ways.

Money is a tool to create the life you want. People face many obstacles, and while some are external, many are related to internal money blocks that stand in the way of clarity and confidence. To move forward, you must shift your mindset and clear what keeps you stuck in your pattern. Whether you are single, married, divorced or widowed, retired or still working, taking control of your finances and finding the confidence to create transformation isn't just about moving this money here or signing this form there.

If you only focus on the nuts and bolts but neglect the internal issues, (your money blocks) you'll find yourself in the same place over and over again—overwhelmed, unsure, and unheard. Wealth alone will not give you fulfillment or make you feel in control if your internal scripts are filled with negative self-doubts. You may continue to accumulate debt even after having just worked your way out of it.

The good news is that once you clear the money blocks that are holding you back from reaching your financial goals, you can live the life you want. You will have more money as well as the confidence in your ability to make financial decisions. You will be able to talk about money openly with the right advisor so he or she can help you reach your goals faster. You will learn to prioritize your needs over others instead of the other way around so you aren't, for example, jeopardizing your retirement to pay for your kid's college. It doesn't have to be an either-or dilemma.

The five biggest money blocks that people face are (i) prioritizing the needs of others over your own, (ii) money secrecy, (iii) lacking confidence in your own knowledge, (iv) uncertainty and decision paralysis, and (v) lacking trustworthy financial advice. (Snappy Kraken, 2020). Grab a notebook and pen, and let's take a look at how each one of these blocks could potentially show up in our lives.

Prioritizing the Needs of Others over Your Own

Do any of the following sound like you?

- I don't take time for myself because I don't want to be selfish.
- I sometimes give more money than I can afford for weddings, birthdays, etc.
- I show my love by giving gifts or money.
- I don't feel worthy unless I'm doing things for other people.
- Anything extra I have, I give to my kids or loved ones; they deserve it more than I do.
- I don't like spending money on myself.

If these sound familiar, then prioritizing the needs of others over your own is a block for you. These thoughts simply aren't true. The truth is you must put on your own oxygen mask before helping others. Showing up for others as your best self starts with you taking care of you.

Let's uncover the origin of this block together. Open your notebook and answer the following questions. Take some time to reflect and be honest with yourself.

1. What does this internal monologue tell you about your value to others?
2. Where do these thoughts about yourself come from?
3. What would it mean for you to put yourself on equal footing with others?

Now that you have your answers, let's replace this block with what you would like to believe instead. For example, if you find it difficult to take time for yourself, tell yourself, "I value myself enough to be the first priority in my life. This isn't selfish. This is loving me in the best, healthiest way. It's about establishing boundaries and standing in my own power. When I do this, I am fulfilled, and that enables me to give to others from a place of strength rather than weakness because I feel I have, too."

Think of one small action you can take today to put yourself first. It could be as simple as sitting in your favorite chair outside with a cup of coffee and reading your book for however long you'd like. You get the point. The truth is when we take care of ourselves first, we have more to give to others. Instead of some worn out tired version, they are getting the best version of us!

Money Secrecy

Shh! Money secrecy is our next block that may be an issue for some of you. Your parents may have taught you it's taboo to talk about money to others, that it's a private matter. Or maybe they never discussed money with you, so you stay quiet during money conversations because you don't know what to say. You may find it hard to open up about money with your partner for fear of being judged. Maybe you don't talk about it with your siblings because you feel they may ask to you to borrow money if they know how much you have.

I never knew how much money my dad made, but I remember my mom saying, "If you find a guy half as good as your dad, you will be okay." As a little girl, I took that to mean the husband brings home the money and the wife manages it. That doesn't work so well in today's time as usually two incomes are needed to provide for the family. Luckily, I was always ambitious and didn't accept the idea that a man was a financial plan. I hope after reading this book you won't either. It is so important for women to be financially independent because you never know what could happen. Things can change in an instant. It's better to be prepared than sorry.

Here are some the symptoms of a money secrecy block:

- I find it hard to open up about money with my partner or loved ones.
- I don't talk about how I spend my money.
- I stay quiet during conversations about money because I don't know what to say.
- I dislike talking about money, salary, or other financial topics.
- I think money is a taboo topic.
- I don't like talking to financial professionals because I don't feel heard.
- My partner and I are not on the same page about money.
- Money makes me anxious.

Ladies, did you know that staying silent about money contributes to lower salaries for you in the workplace? It also contributes to the common myth that women aren't as good with money as men.

In order to bring these blocks from our subconscious mind to our conscious mind, it's important to write everything down. Then it can be healed and released. So, write your answers to the following questions in your notebook.

1. What is the first thought that pops into your head when you think about money?
2. When did you start believing this?
3. Where did this belief come from?

Now, ask yourself what you would like to believe instead. For example, if you are struggling to share your finances with your partner, tell yourself, "I am great at handling money. But by working with my partner, we combine both of our money skills sets, and we both feel heard and valued by each other. We both know where we stand financially and are better able to make financial decisions together. We are on the same team, and we reach our goals faster because we don't have any secrets. As a result, our relationship has also improved." Today, you can take action by opening up to your partner about your hesitation to discuss money. Baby steps go a long way. If you and your partner can talk openly about money, it will allow space for communication in other areas of your relationship as well.

Lacking Confidence in Your Own Knowledge

How many of you are overwhelmed when you think of your finances and goals? Do you think you should know more about money at this point in your life? Do you tell yourself you're just not good with numbers, and you'll never understand them? These are signs of block number three, lacking confidence in your own knowledge.

More symptoms of this block include the following:
- I'm afraid I'll ask stupid questions.
- I feel intimidated when people use investment jargon.
- I feel judged when I open up about money.
- I don't feel heard by financial professionals.
- I feel guilty about how I manage my money.

It doesn't have to be this way. For those looking to learn new things about money or how to handle your finances, reading this book is a good start to increasing your knowledge! For others, it will be a confidence booster to confirm what you already know.

Let's get to the source of this block. Answer the following in your notebook.

1. Why do you believe these things?
2. Where did this script come from?

To clear this block, simply replace it with what you would like to believe instead. What little thing can you do today to counteract this block? For example, if you always believed you weren't good with numbers, change that belief to "I am good with numbers, and I also have my calculator to verify." Today, you can take action by tallying all your current monthly expenses to see how much money you already have saved in your emergency fund. (I recommend six months of expenses if you have a single source of income or three months if you are a part of a two-household income. But always do what makes you feel secure if an emergency should arise.)

Uncertainty and Decision Paralysis

These days, this block is very common because of all the available information we are bombarded with on a daily basis. You may suffer from this block if you find yourself saying the following:

- I know I need to make changes to my finances, but I don't know where to start.
- I've talked to a financial professional, and I went away even more confused.
- I'm not sure what my options are or what decisions I need to make.
- I feel overwhelmed when I think about my finances.
- I have to optimize every choice, or I'll fail.
- Retirement is so far away. I don't need to worry about it now.
- Retirement is so close that nothing I do will change anything now.

The truth is you don't need to know all the answers before taking action. You can decide to start saving for retirement, and then seek out a trusted professional to help guide your through all the different options to find the best one for you.

Take a deeper look into what your internal monologue is telling you about this block. Write down everything that comes to mind, and don't censor yourself. You are the only one who will read what you wrote.

1. When did you start believing these things?
2. Where did it come from?

Now that you got all of those reasons out of your system, let them go. Tell yourself, "If I didn't have to be 100% correct about every decision, I would stop procrastinating. I would start saving and investing what I could now. The more time I have to save and invest the more time my money has to compound and grow. If I wait until some point in the future, I can never get that time back. I know I can find an advisor to put me on the right path, help me avoid costly mistakes, and they can simplify my finances for me. That's what they get paid for." Today, you can take action by being conscious of your thoughts. Anytime something pops into your head that stops you from moving forward in your finances, pause and find out where this is coming from. Then, counteract that negative thought with a small action you can take to move forward in the right direction.

Lacking Trustworthy Financial Advice

This last block is a huge one. It *must* be overcome because it will hold you back from reaching your goals and fulfilling your dreams. Research shows that working with a financial professional adds three percent to your bottom line. (Vanguard, 2019) Symptoms of this block are as follows:

- I don't think the financial industry is trustworthy.
- I feel bombarded by information, and it's all conflicting.
- I don't have anyone I can trust to talk to about money.

- I don't think I have enough money to get professional advice.
- I'm not sure which source of information I can trust.
- Markets are rigged, so I'd rather not do anything risky.

Working with a professional is one of the smartest things you can do with your money. It is so much more than your portfolio. A professional is there to serve as your mentor, behavioral coach, and accountability partner.

Go back to your notebook and answer the following questions.

1. If you believe any of the statements above to be true, why do you feel that way?
2. Where did this belief come from?
3. Did you have a bad experience in the past?

Let's replace this block by being honest with yourself. What kind of advice do you need? If you're unsure, that's okay! Write down that you don't know. What is one small action you can take today to counteract this block? Maybe you call a financial professional to set up an interview and see if there is a synergy between you two. If not, keep calling other professionals until you find one you are comfortable with.

There are many other blocks around money, but these five are the most common. Write your answers to the following steps for any other blocks you may come across.

1. Why you believe what you believe about the block
2. Where you think it came from
3. What you would like to believe instead
4. One small step you can take to counteract the block

If you do this whenever you encounter any block, I promise your life will improve dramatically. You will be more fulfilled and have more abundance in your life!

6. How to Invest Your Money in the Market—What Works and What Doesn't

Investing in the stock market doesn't have to be complicated, although the financial services industry doesn't want you to know this. They develop all of these complicated strategies and package them to be the latest, greatest product or strategy you need in order to reach your goals. I believe they develop them for job security. These complicated strategies may be good for a few people like the super wealthy, but most people just need a simple, proven strategy that will help them reach their financial goals.

With the simple strategy I am going to teach you, it may look like your advisor is not doing much to earn their fee, but that is farthest from the truth! If you feel your advisor has to be buying and selling all the time, moving in and out of cash, trying to beat the market, or otherwise question why you are paying your advisor, this may be a block. Follow the steps from the previous chapter to clear the block and avoid hurting your future goals.

Evidence-Based Investing

Let me ask you a question. Would you rather: (i) gamble with your retirement money and take unnecessary risks (based on your feelings or what the so called "experts" say), or (ii) use a simple, proven strategy that takes the guesswork out of investing for your retirement and future goals? Right, I'm going with the second option as well.

I believe in the evidence-based investing philosophy. Evidence can clear the path for investing success and show us certain risks are not worth taking. Evidence has positively impacted results in nearly every aspect of our lives. What does evidence do? It supports theory.

For many years, people thought the earth was flat and they could fall off its edge until it was proven through scientific evidence that the

29

earth is, in fact, round. It sounds ridiculous today, but when we get something in our head or someone tells us something, we automatically believe it until it's proven otherwise. Once science progressed, we were able to change our beliefs and see the truth.

How about evidence in medicine? When I was a kid, we didn't wear helmets when riding our bikes, but today, no parent would dare let their child ride a bike without a helmet. Why is that? Did my parents love me any less? Of course not! In 2017, a study was done by the Bicycle Safety Institute, and they found that almost three-quarters of fatal crashes (74%) involved a head injury. Nearly all bicyclists who died (97%) were not wearing a helmet. (Bicycle Helmet Safety Institute, 2017) With this new evidence, people could see that riding a bike without a helmet isn't safe.

Finally, let's take a look at how evidence in law changed the way crimes were solved. Back in the 1930s, there was no DNA testing, so detectives solved cases based on hunches. Can you imagine how many innocent people were wrongfully accused? I would never want to be accused of a crime, but especially not in those days! Once DNA testing became available, cold cases were reopened and solved, and innocent people were freed after years of being locked up for crimes they did not commit. As you can see, evidence reveals the truth about a situation.

Without evidence, investors can be lured into making harmful investing decisions. As I mentioned earlier, most investors do not make their investment decisions based on the evidence. They make decisions based on emotions. They try to time the market, pick individual stocks, chase manager performance, and manage their own portfolio.

Market Timing

Market timing is the act of moving in and out of the market or switching between asset classes based on using predictive methods. Many technical analysts rely on charts and look for the support and resistance levels. Once the market goes above or below these levels, they make a move with their portfolio. In order to trade this way, an investor would have to know exactly when the market has hit the bottom and when it's hit its peak.

The cover of the March 9, 2009 edition of *Time Magazine* had a photo of hands clenching a breaking rope. The headline read, "Holding on for Dear Life." Now, some people who saw that in the supermarket checkout line might have thought, "Oh no, this isn't looking good! The market is going to keep dropping. I better move the money I have invested to cash and wait until things get better." If they did that, they would have been very disappointed. The day that edition came out was the bottom in the market and marked the beginning of recovery from the financial crisis. The stock market rose from there.

We saw history repeat itself on March 23, 2020. The stock market was at its low. Again, some people panicked and moved to cash and they missed out on the stock market rebound and the market continued to set record highs. Even if you knew ahead of time that in 2020 we would have a pandemic and social and political unrest, you probably would not have predicted that, on January 1st, the stock market would rise to a record high. You most likely would have assumed the market was going crash and stay down.

Of course, not all investors think this way, and for every seller there is a buyer. As Warren Buffett said, "Buy when there is blood in the streets." When you see a good stock at garage sale prices, that is the time to buy more, not sell.

So, is there evidence for buying more when the market is down (or at least not selling at that time)? Figure 1 illustrates what would have happened if you had $100,000 and kept it invested in certain indexes from September 2008 to December 2019.

Figure 1

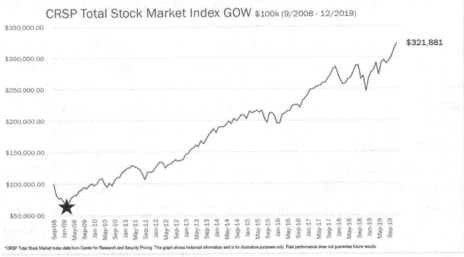

In 1990, William F. Sharpe, a professor of finance at Stanford University, was awarded the Nobel Prize for Economics for his work in developing models to help with investment decisions. In 1975, he published an article, "Likely Gains from Market Timing," that proved statistically that a trader would have to guess right 74% of the time to benefit from a market timing strategy.

Figure 2 summarizes would have happened if you had $10,000 and remained fully invested from December 31, 1994 until December 31, 2004. You would have more than tripled your initial investment. On the other hand, if you tried to time the market, you would have experienced much less growth and most likely had negative returns. That's because you have to be right 74% of time. I don't like those odds!

Figure 2

Missing the Market[1]
S&P 500 Index: December 31, 1994 – December 31, 2004

Period of Investment	Average Annual Total Return	Growth of $10,000
Fully invested	12.07%	$31,260
Missed the 10 best days	6.89	19,476
Missed the 20 best days	2.89	13,414
Missed the 30 best days	-.39	9,621
Missed the 40 best days	-3.19	7,233
Missed the 60 best days	-7.90	4,390

[1] FactSet Research Systems Inc.

Picking Individual Stocks

There are some people who dream of striking it rich by picking stocks. They hear how others have made millions doing this, and they want in on it. If this is you, I'm sorry to burst your bubble, but this isn't a winning strategy for your hard earned money and the success of your future goals. Being successful with this strategy is similar to winning the lottery. There is more luck than skill involved, and the chances are extremely slim that you will be correct in the long term.

Investors aren't alone in this line of thinking, though. Many advisors also attempt to build portfolios with individual stocks based on predictive measures. Let's look at how the financial experts from different money magazines did in 2016. They each had their "best stocks" list. If you followed the list from MSN or InvestorPlace, you would have earned 2.3% that year. *Kiplinger's* list earned 3.7%. The stock picks from *Time* and *Money Magazine* (which isn't even around anymore) earned 4.9%. *Barron's* had the best performing stock picks out of all of them, earning 5.3%. If you would have saved all the money you had spent on those magazines and invested in the Center for Research in the Security Prices (CSRP) Total Stock Market Index you would have earned 12.83%! (Darlin, 2017)

There is a game I like to play at my live events. I fill up a Mason jar with 500 jellybeans to represent the stocks of the S&P 500 index. Every year, approximately 300 of these stocks underperform the index. (Bessembinder, 2017) In the Mason jar, I mix 300 BeanBoozled jellybeans (the ones with flavors like toothpaste or stinky socks) with 200 delicious jellybeans. I ask for a volunteer to see if he or she can pick a good one. Some get lucky, but about 60% of the time, they end up spitting out the jellybean.

When I first tried, I got a really bad jellybean. I think it was dog food. It was so gross I had to spit it out, wash my mouth out, and drink something. But I was glad that wasn't a mistake made with my hard-earned money! This jellybean example is like trying to pick the winning stocks, but when you make a bad stock pick, you have more than just a bad taste in your mouth. At the end of the event I give out a small container with four good and six bad jellybeans so they can share this exercise with their kids and friends. It's a great teaching moment.

If you need another reason to avoid investing in individual stocks, let's not forget about some of the biggest bankruptcies in history: Enron, CIT (a bank holding company), GM, World Com, Washington Mutual, and Lehman Brothers. These were solid companies at one point, but they ended up losing billions and then went bankrupt. No one could have predicted this would happen to such successful companies. Once again, the evidence states we should not try to pick stocks. Jack Bogle, the founder of The Vanguard Group, said, "Don't look for the needle in the haystack. Just buy the haystack." In other words, buy the whole market not individual stocks.

Chasing Manager Performance

At this point, you might be thinking, "I know I can't time the markets or pick individual stocks, but I can find those who can in advance." I'm happy that you get the first part, but I'm going to have to burst your bubble once again. Past performance is no guarantee of future results. Investors have heard that time and time again, but they don't believe it! It is true, which is why it's required on every piece of financial literature.

Here is a perfect example. In August 2006, Bill Miller, Legg Mason's fund manager, was touted by *Smart Money Magazine* as one of the "World's Greatest Investors." During the financial crisis in 2008, he snapped up AIG, Wachovia, Bear Stearns, and Freddie Mac. The latter three were almost wiped out, and Miller rode them all the way down. Even the best money manager couldn't replicate his success.

Figure 3 shows us very few money managers can repeat their past performance in the second year. In 2007 and 2008, no money manager could.

Figure 3

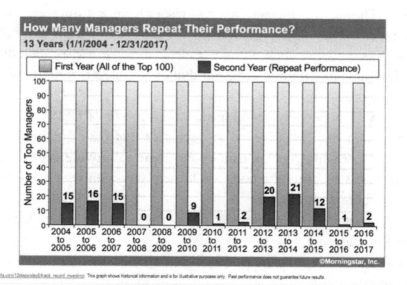

Many people make their investment decisions based on what forecasters say. You know, like the talking heads on TV. But often, they're wrong and can destroy wealth. In a *Fortune* magazine article entitled, "Confessions of a Mutual Fund Reporter," an anonymous author wrote:

By day we write 'Six Funds to Buy NOW!' ...By night, however, we invest in sensible index funds... Unfortunately, rational, pro-index-fund stories don't sell magazines, cause hits on Websites [sic], or boost Nielsen ratings. So rest assured: You'll keep on seeing those enticing but worthless SIX FUNDS TO BUY NOW! headlines as long as there are personal-finance media. (Fortune Magazine, 1999)

Wow! Evidence straight from the source. As you can see, chasing a manager's past performance does not guarantee you success.

Managing Your Own Portfolio

The best way to reach your financial goals with peace of mind is to follow the evidence-based investing philosophy and work with a CFP®. The biggest impact we as advisors have is to prevent you from making emotional decisions which could cost you thousands of dollars or more. Yes, you can open up an e-trade account or use a robo-advisor to buy investments on your own, but this only works if you know exactly what you are doing.

As I previously mentioned, working with a CFP® adds 3% to your bottom line. There are also strategies that only qualified advisors can help you with, such as using your home to provide tax-free income in retirement or using the tax code to help you with your cash flow and tax-free retirement income.

Being able to call up your advisor is a benefit to you because you have a relationship with this advisor. They know you and your goals and are concerned about your well-being. You can open up to them about your situation. The more information your advisor has the better they can help you.

Using a robo-advisor takes the human element out of financial planning. A robo-advisor only focuses on the numbers. Do you want to call up an 800 number and get a different person every time you have a question? How comfortable are you going to be in sharing your financial situation with a different stranger each time you call? Without consistent help from the same person who knows your situation, it can be hard to navigate the complexities of finances. You may even end up costing yourself thousands of dollars because of mistakes that could be avoided with an advisor's help.

For example, what would happen if you logged into your online account to do a Roth conversion (we'll talk more later in the book about what this is), and you accidentally converted your entire $2 million dollar IRA instead of $20,000? This mistake will cost you $740,000 in federal income taxes if you are in a 37% tax bracket! You might think, "No biggie. I'll just call up the 800 number and tell them my mistake so they can fix it." However, under the current laws, once you do a Roth conversion, there is no do over like there used to be.

If you worked with an advisor, they would have looked at your entire financial situation and determined whether a Roth conversion made sense for you before executing this transaction in the first place. And if it did, he or she would have chosen the correct amount to convert.

Why Evidence-Based Investing Works

Now that we know what doesn't work when it comes to investing our money, let's evaluate what does work. This evidence is going to be critical for your investing success. Evidence-based investing eliminates market timing, picking individual stocks, and chasing manager performance by incorporating Nobel Prize-winning academic theories about how markets work.

The first theory is the Efficient Market Hypothesis. This states that the markets are priced correctly. The price that a stock is trading at today is a fair price, and no one can take advantage of mispricing. The next component is market factors. You want to own small companies as well as value companies.

Another theory incorporated into evidence-based investing is the Modern Portfolio Theory. This theory is based on a diversified portfolio where returns are maximized based on risk level. Finally, you want to understand behavior and avoid emotional investing decisions.

Efficient Market Hypothesis

If you can't beat the markets, what should you do? Join them! They are really great wealth creation tools. Figure 4 illustrates different market returns by asset class in comparison to inflation.

Figure 4

Asset	Return (1/1994 – 12/2019)
S&P 500	9.86%
5 Year US Government Treasury Bonds	4.72%
One-Month Treasury Bills	2.38%
Inflation	2.21%

*S&P 500 Index data from Standard and Poors Financial Services, Five Year US Gov't Treasury Bonds and One-month Treasury Bills Data from United States Treasury. Inflation data from United States Federal Reserve. This graph shows historical information and is for illustrative purposes only. Past performance does not guarantee future results.

The goal of investing is to outpace inflation, which treasury bills barely did during this time period. Inflation erodes your wealth and your spending power. This is because your money is worth less tomorrow than it is today. The market did well, and as you become more conservative and take less risk, you can expect a smaller return.

Most people think that it is impossible to accumulate a million dollars in their lifetime. This isn't true. You all can accumulate at least one million dollars in your lifetime, making you a millionaire, if you save and invest appropriately. Don't speculate and gamble. Figure 5 shows how this is possible.

Figure 5

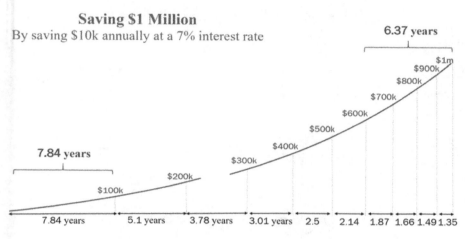

Saving $1 Million
By saving $10k annually at a 7% interest rate

Note: used with permission from Evidence Based Advisors, ©2020.

Let's assume you invest $10,000 a year and earn 7%. The first $100,000 is the hardest to accumulate. Due to compounding interest, it takes 7.84 years. Einstein was right when he called compounding interest the eighth wonder of the world! The next $100,000 takes only 5.1 years due to compounding interest. The last $400,000 takes less time to accumulate than the first $100,000! Thank you compounding interest!

Market Factors and the Modern Portfolio Theory

Why do we want to include small companies in our portfolios? Because all large companies started out as small companies. Apple, Amazon, Facebook and Google all started out in someone's garage or college dorm room. Small companies have higher expected returns and can greatly diversify a portfolio. Look at the evidence illustrated in Figure 6.

Figure 6

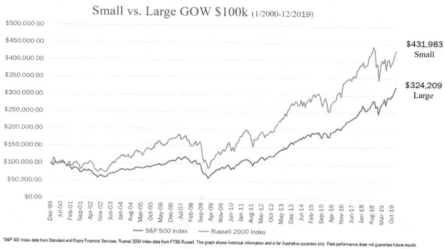

Small vs. Large GOW $100k (1/2000-12/2019)

Value companies are distressed for some reason or another. Then, they become growth companies someday after they get healthier. This provides higher expected returns. Some big-name companies were once distressed and have seen a lot of growth over the years. Apple almost went out of business in the 90s, Nintendo in the early 2000s, Delta in the mid-2000s, Starbucks in 2008, and Netflix in 2011. No one knows which company is going to go from distressed to growth, which is why you should own them all. In Figure 7, we see the evidence to support why value companies should be added to the portfolio.

Figure 7

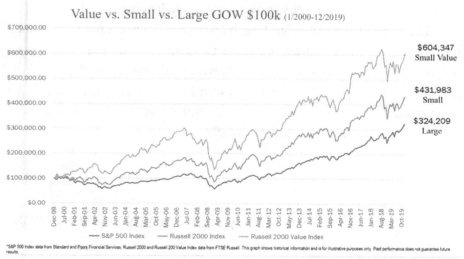

Value vs. Small vs. Large GOW $100k (1/2000-12/2019)

$604,347
Small Value

$431,983
Small

$324,209
Large

— S&P 500 Index   — Russell 2000 Index   — Russell 2000 Value Index

S&P 500 Index data from Standard and Poors Financial Services, Russell 2000 and Russell 200 Value Index data from FTSE Russell. This graph shows historical information and is for illustrative purposes only. Past performance does not guarantee future results.

Again, you want to stay diversified and have small, value, and large companies in your portfolio. Diversification is your friend. You don't want to put all your eggs in one basket. Meaning you don't want to invest all your money in one stock, one sector, or one country.

Avoiding Emotional Investing Decisions with the Help of a Financial Planner

You are most likely your worst enemy when it comes to investing because it's your hard-earned money, and you are so attached to it. This is why it's so important to work with a trusted advisor to help you navigate the cycle of emotions you will go through. Markets don't go up in a straight line. There are ups and downs along the way. It's like an emotional rollercoaster.

When the market is going up, people get excited. They hear on the news about all-time market highs, and now, they are really excited and want in. So, they invest, and then, the market drops. And drops. And drops some more. People get really worried and panic and then sell at the bottom. And the cycle starts again. Most investors buy high and sell low because of emotions. In reality, you want to buy low and sell high.

Humans have 188 cognitive biases that have been around since the beginning of time. These biases will destroy your portfolio. Your perception of reality based on your experiences dictates your behavior. A trusted advisor is going to take the emotions out of investing and keep you invested so you can reach your financial goals. Look at Figure 8 to see the emotions an investor goes through.

Figure 8

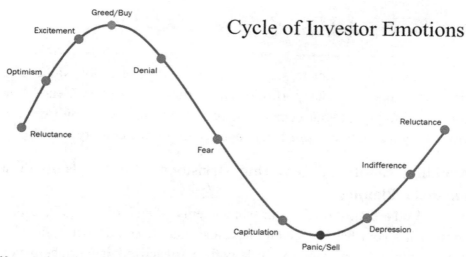

Note: used with permission from Evidence Based Advisors, ©2020.

Figure 9 further proves the point that investors make emotional decisions.

Figure 9

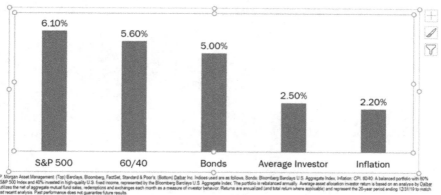

Diversification and the Average Investor
1999-2019 (20 Years)

S&P 500	60/40	Bonds	Average Investor	Inflation
6.10%	5.60%	5.00%	2.50%	2.20%

*Source: J.P. Morgan Asset Management (Top) Barclays, Bloomberg, FactSet, Standard & Poor's. (Bottom) Dalbar Inc. Indices used are as follows, Bonds: Bloomberg Barclays U.S. Aggregate Index, Inflation: CPI. 60/40: A balanced portfolio with 60% invested in S&P 500 Index and 40% invested in high-quality U.S. fixed income, represented by the Bloomberg Barclays U.S. Aggregate Index. The portfolio is rebalanced annually. Average asset allocation investor return is based on an analysis by Dalbar Inc., which utilizes the net of aggregate mutual fund sales, redemptions and exchanges each month as a measure of investor behavior. Returns are annualized (and total return where applicable) and represent the 20-year period ending 12/31/19 to match Dalbar's most recent analysis. Past performance does not guarantee future results.

Here you see that the average investor barely beats inflation—more evidence that proves by working with an advisor, we add 3% to your bottom line. Why not live your life doing what you do best, enjoying time with your family and friends, and not worrying about figuring out how to invest in the market?

Most people speculate and gamble. Even if you did have the knowledge to invest, most people don't have a handle on these scary emotions that will come up time and time again. As your account balances grow, fear starts to creep in, and you will very likely succumb to your emotions. Even the most sophisticated investor will succumb to his or her emotions at some point.

In March 2020, I had a client who claimed he had information that no one else knew about the economic conditions and that the market was headed for a crash, so he wanted to move his portfolio to cash. He kept saying it's going to get even worse. Since the writing of this chapter, the market has recovered, and my clients are positive for the year. Fortunately, he didn't move to cash. If he did, he would have missed out on the recovery. No one knows the precise time of when to get in and when to get out of the market. Let yourself sleep at night and have the financial peace of mind that comes with relying on evidence and professional help instead of going it alone.

7. Moving to Cash Is the Worst Thing You Can Do to Your Portfolio

When markets are volatile, people get scared. When they turn on the news, they become even more afraid of investing. The worst thing you can do during volatile times is to move your portfolio to cash. By doing this, you can be certain of one thing: you have locked in your losses.

You heard the cliché it's only a paper loss. While that is correct, humans don't like to suffer any loss, perceived or real. As we learned in chapter five, this is just another money block that needs to be cleared. If you suffer from this block, put this book down right now, grab a piece of paper, and follow the steps I taught to you to release it before reading on any further.

I had somebody call me during a period of volatility, and he wanted me to manage his retirement savings, which he wasn't planning on using for another thirteen years. He had been managing it on his own but kept losing money. He would gain some, then the market would go down, and he'd get scared and move it to cash. The day after we signed the paperwork, the market was down 600 points. He was sitting in cash but wanted me to wait before I invested his account because he thought the market would go down further.

First of all, accounts don't move immediately. The firm sending the money and the receiving firm each have to review all paperwork. Second, the market was up the very next day. It doesn't matter when you invest because time in the market is more important than trying to time the market.

I explained to my client that this is what he had been doing all along, which is how he arrived at his current position. Now that he had me, he had a strategy. I found out what his emotional risk score was, and I built a low-cost portfolio around that number. We would stay invested in the good times and bad times, and we would take advantage of the bad times by rebalancing.

Rebalancing is when you bring the portfolio back into alignment with its original design. We either buy or sell a portion of each holding so that the resulting percentage of the portfolio invested in each holding is in line with prior allocations. By doing so, we basically buy low and sell high.

Nobody can time the market because nobody has a crystal ball. In 2015, CNBC gave an example of a really bad market timer. An investor (let's call him Bob) began investing in 1973 over what would be forty-two-year time horizon. He put $6,000 into the S&P 500 before the market dropped 48%. He was upset, but he stayed invested, although he didn't deposit any more money into his account until he felt comfortable again. He was brave enough right before the 1987 crash, and he deposited $46,000 into his account, which was what he had saved up to that point. After that crash, he was feeling really bad again, and he didn't get back into the market until 2000 when he put $68,000 into his account only to watch it crash in 2001. Bob had the worst luck! In 2007, he put in another $64,000, and we all know what happened in 2008. The market crashed yet again! But before you start feeling sorry for poor Bob, let's look at the amount of money he ended up with.

Over the forty-two years, he invested a total of $184,000. During that time, it grew to $1.6 million dollars! That is a total return of about 9%. His profit was $980,000! You are probably scratching your head right now wondering how this happened. After all, Bob had the worst luck, and every time he invested, the market crashed shortly thereafter.

His profit was the result of staying invested and not moving his portfolio to cash when he got scared. If history teaches us one thing, it is that the market always recovers. The best time to invest is today. No one knows when the market is going to be at its peak or bottom until after it has occurred.

Now, let's look at a twenty-year time horizon of investing in the S&P 500 from 1999 to 2018 using information from a 2019 study from Capital Group/American Funds. Let's say an investor got in on the best days, meaning the market was at its low point each year, and he put $10,000 in every year for those twenty years. In December 2018 at the end of twenty years, he would have $546,793, which is a 9.16% average annual rate of return.

Let's say another investor also put in $10,000 a year over the same time horizon, but this investor put his money in on the worst days when the market was at its all-time high for that year. This person had a 6.91% average annual rate of return and ended up with a balance of $415,460.

They both experienced positive returns because they didn't move to cash when the market became volatile during times of the tech bubble and the housing crisis that led to the 2008 recession. Time in the market—not trying to time the market—is what is important. Just get in and hold on.

Your friends at work might be saying, "Oh, I moved my money to cash, and then I put money in this fund, and my account is up 20%." That is luck, and luck is not a long-term strategy. In order to get the same return as your friend, you would have had to put your money into the market at the same time they did. If you were to put your money in now—after your friend already received their return—it would be too late. You would not receive the same return they did. This is not the way to go about investing for your future, which is why I stress the importance of working with a CFP®.

If you want to invest your money with me, the first thing I do is determine your risk tolerance. I find your emotional risk score, which is going to tell me what you really feel. I need that information because we're going to talk about your actual numbers, and then we're going to build a portfolio to match that number.

When the markets are doing well, life is great. But when we experience volatility, you have me to reassure you that your plan is on track and to remind you that we have prepared for this when we first determined your risk number. This is where I earn my keep. I'm not going to let you run to cash. I'm going to hold your hand through it all, giving you that financial peace of mind because I'm here to help you reach your financial goals. I do that by teaching you to take the emotions out of investing and being a partner so you don't have to do it on your own any longer.

Vanguard did a study showing that by working with a financial advisor, we add 3% to your bottom line. You will more than make up for our fee, which is nominal compared to what you would lose by investing on your own. In fact, many do-it-yourself investors have had negative returns.

For the past ninety-one years, the S&P 500 has ups and downs every year. About twenty-seven of those years had negative results in a one-year time frame, meaning if you went out to cash in one year and didn't stay invested, you would have really lost twenty-seven of those years. Now, if you stayed invested for just three years, you would have experienced half of those negative year periods. If you went out for ten years, you would only experience five of those negative periods.

I cannot stress enough how important it is to stay in the market. That might seem like the risky thing to do, but all the evidence has shown that if you stay in the market, you get the reward.

8. Spending Plans (Because Budgeting Is a Dirty Word)

Many people think if they just earn more money, they will be financially stable. That is simply not true. How many of you save the raises you receive each year? If you do, then I want to congratulate you! This is a great step toward seeking financial stability. The problem with most people, though, is when we make more money, we spend more money. That does not provide financial stability or help us build wealth. Even if you make six or seven figures a year, you can still be broke!

It doesn't have to be this way if you start saving early instead of spending everything you make. This is how you build wealth instead of giving off the appearance that you are wealthy. No matter your income level, you can have financial stability.

The answer is simple: live below your means. Don't spend everything you make. Pay down credit card debt, build an emergency fund, stick to a financial plan, save for retirement, and protect your earnings with life and disability insurance. With every paycheck, pay yourself first. No matter what stage of life you are in, you can be financially secure.

The first step to financial stability is to know where you stand. If you don't know where you are, it's hard to get to your destination. Take an inventory of your assets, your income, and your expenses. If you find that you have more expenses than income, it's time to start reevaluating your priorities and choices.

Ideally, you would want to save 20% of your income. If that is not possible, aim for 10% to start and work your way up to that number. Every time you get a paycheck, save 20% before you spend the rest. In other words, pay yourself first. If you are saving 5% into your retirement plan at work, then you can save 15%, although I still recommend 20% if possible. The 20% will go to building your emergency fund, your short-term goals, and your long-term goals, such as retirement. After you've put your 20% in savings, you have 80% left to live off of, so you make it work. Maybe that means you eat out once a week instead of twice.

Some people feel they need more structure in their spending plan. A popular spending plan is the **50%/30%/20% plan**. Here, 50% is spent on needs, which is anything you need to live and survive. This includes housing, medical, utilities (just the essential like gas and electric), and groceries. 30% goes to wants. This includes extras in life that make you happy like dining out, cell phone bills, pets, internet and subscription services, shopping, entertainment, vacations, gifting and charitable donations, and luxury car purchases vs. a basic car to get you from point A to point B. The final 20% goes to debt repayment and savings (short and long-term). Depending on where you live and what you make, you may have to adjust these numbers slightly.

If you like to have more detail, you can use the **zero-sum spending plan**. This is good for people who earn a living on commissions or have irregular income. This plan requires that you think about every dollar you spend. Using last month's income, assign each dollar to this month's expenses. You must give every dollar "a job" to prevent waste and maximize your income with the ultimate goal of reaching zero at the end of the month. You should have one month of expenses saved before you start using this method. If you have excess, assign it somewhere, such as an extra debt payment or extra savings that month. If you don't assign the excess, it usually gets spent and wasted. If your income fluctuates, use your lowest income month or take the average over the last twelve months.

When deciding which spending plan to use, it's important to pick one that is going to work for you. If you are debt-free except for your mortgage and want something easy, saving 20% and then living on 80% is a good choice. If you have a lot of debt and need to curb wasteful spending and get back on track, the zero-sum spending plan may work best for you. If you are still operating in the scarcity mindset and have a hard time spending money for your wants, the 50/30/20 plan may work for you. Hopefully, you are using the abundance prayer and clearing your blocks so this isn't a problem for long. The bottom line is implement one of these spending plans and stick with it so you can have financial stability.

9. Getting Out of Debt and Staying Out!

Finding ourselves in debt can happen to anyone, wealthy or not. There are many reasons why people find themselves in debt: divorce, unforeseen medical expenses, sudden death of a spouse who didn't have enough life insurance. Most of these are events that you can't control. (Buying the proper amount of insurance is in your control, but many people are blocked around that.) I want to focus on the reasons that we go into debt that *are* in our control. Unless we uncover the real reasons we are in debt and we face these demons, we will find ourselves in debt over and over again. It's best to deal with *why* we're in debt before we go into the process of how to get out of it.

Why Am I in Debt?

You might overspend because you grew up poor and were told you couldn't have something because it wasn't affordable. So, when you grew up and got a job, you wanted to spoil yourself because you sacrificed a lot, and now you want all the things you couldn't have when you were younger. Maybe you want to appear successful to others in order to seek their approval. So, you go out and buy a lot of stuff to keep up with the Joneses. Pretty soon, you are thousands of dollars in debt and feel even worse than you did before you had all that stuff.

In both of these scenarios, debt was created to fill an internal void. Stuff isn't going to make you happy. You must go within to find true happiness. Clearing our blocks and facing our shadows and demons is what will truly set us on the path to being debt-free.

I'm in the financial planning profession, I graduated at the top of my class, and I've made poor choices with my money which put me in debt. At some point in our lives, we all will make a bad choice or decision with our money. Mine was that I went into debt in the name of love (or rather, because I wanted this person to love me). I'm smart enough to know that money can't buy love. But because I didn't love myself in the healthiest and best way, I ended up making decisions based on emotions instead of reason. It's like an addiction—it can happen to anyone.

I was twenty-one and in love with this guy who was thirty-six. He told a sob story about how he lost faith in love since his divorce, and he believed he would never love again. Well, I was on a mission to make him love me and prove to him that love exists. He definitely was not worthy of my love. It was an emotionally abusive relationship to say the least, and basically, I became his Sugar Mama.

Needless to say, I spent all my money on him and let him have free reign of my credit card. After I finally smartened up a few years later and had suffered enough, I was $36,000 in debt! My parents offered to pay off my debts and put me through school to get my Master's degree in education. At the time, I couldn't see their generosity. I thought they were trying to control me and run my life, and my stubbornness and pride would not allow that. I didn't want to be a teacher! I was going to be a star! Besides, I had a finance degree for my back up plan. I also believed I had to punish myself. Since I had gotten myself into this mess in the first place, I had to get myself out of it.

That is just what I did. I only had a salary of $26,000 at the time, so I bartended every Friday and Saturday until 4:00 a.m. for a year straight. It was hard work, but I was determined, and I was debt free in a year. Every extra penny I made went to repaying my debt. I was so proud of myself.

We are all human and money is an emotional subject. No woman should have to experience what I went through, so I want you to know that you are enough and perfect the way you are. The love you are seeking in someone else is already inside of you. Meditate and really connect with that truth, and you will be truly happy.

Methods to Eliminate Debt

There are two methods to reduce debt: the snowball method and the avalanche method. Before we decide on a method that works for you, you should have your list of expenses from when you created your spending plan. Write out a list of each credit card balance with its interest rate, minimum payment, and balance. Figure 10 illustrates what your list might look like.

Figure 10

	Balance	Interest Rate	Minimum Monthly Payment
Chase Card	$945	14.5%	$20
Discover Card	$3000	9.9%	$50
Mastercard	$4600	12.9%	$75

If you prioritize paying off one card at a time instead of reducing overall debt as quickly as possible, the **snowball method** is best for you. It works like this.

1. Arrange your cards from smallest balance to largest balance.
2. Figure out how much extra money you can pay in addition to the minimum payments.
3. Take this extra money and pay it to the card with the smallest balance (the first one on your list.)
4. Pay the minimum payments on the rest of the cards.

5. When the first card is paid off, take everything you paid to the first card and add it to the minimum payment of the card with the next lowest balance.
6. Repeat this until all your credit cards are paid off.

Figure 11 shows the timeline of payments for a person who has $500 a month to pay down this debt.

Figure 11

Debt Snowball Method-pay lowest balance first

#	Month	Chase	Discover	Mastercard	Snowball Amt.	Total Interest	Balance	Total Payment
1	May-21	$375.00	$50.00	$75.00	$355.00	$85.62	$8,545.00	$500.00
2	Jun-21	$375.00	$50.00	$75.00	$355.00	$80.75	$8,130.62	$500.00
3	Jul-21	$213.45	$211.55	$75.00	$375.00	$75.81	$7,711.37	$500.00
4	Aug-21	-	$425.00	$75.00	$375.00	$71.41	$7,284.60	$500.00
5	Sep-21	-	$425.00	$75.00	$375.00	$67.80	$6,856.01	$500.00
6	Oct-21	-	$425.00	$75.00	$375.00	$64.17	$6,423.81	$500.00
7	Nov-21	-	$425.00	$75.00	$375.00	$60.51	$5,987.98	$500.00
8	Dec-21	-	$425.00	$75.00	$375.00	$56.81	$5,548.49	$500.00
9	Jan-22	-	$425.00	$75.00	$375.00	$53.09	$5,105.30	$500.00
10	Feb-22	-	$298.47	$201.53	$425.00	$49.33	$4,658.39	$500.00
11	Mar-22	-	-	$500.00	$425.00	$45.21	$4,205.26	$500.00
12	Apr-22	-	-	$500.00	$425.00	$40.32	$3,750.47	$500.00
13	May-22	-	-	$500.00	$425.00	$35.38	$3,290.79	$500.00
14	Jun-22	-	-	$500.00	$425.00	$30.38	$2,826.17	$500.00
15	Jul-22	-	-	$500.00	$425.00	$25.33	$2,356.55	$500.00
16	Aug-22	-	-	$500.00	$425.00	$20.23	$1,881.88	$500.00
17	Sep-22	-	-	$500.00	$425.00	$15.07	$1,402.11	$500.00
18	Oct-22	-	-	$500.00	$425.00	$9.86	$917.18	$500.00
19	Nov-22	-	-	$427.04	$500.00	$4.59	$427.04	$427.04
20	Dec-22	-	-	-	$500.00	$0.00	$0.00	-
Total Interest Paid						$891.67		

Figure 12 illustrates that by following this method, the total principal and interest paid is $9,427. Total interest paid is $892. Percentage paid in interest is 9.46%. You would be debt free in 1.4 years or 17 months compared to the 8.2 years it would take if you only paid the minimum amount due. Using the snowball method, you are debt free 6.8 years sooner!

Figure 12

Paying Only the Minimum Amount Due	
Total principal & interest:	$13,059
Total Interest:	$4,574
Percentage paid in interest:	35.03%
Years until debt free:	8.2 98 Month(s)
Debt free date:	Aug 2029

Your Selected Payoff Plan	
Total principal & interest:	$9,427
Total interest:	$892
Percentage paid in interest:	9.46%
Years until debt free:	1.4 17 Month(s)
Debt free date:	Nov 2022

Account Payoff Details

Account	Total Payments	Projected Interest	Months to Payoff	Payoff Date
Chase	$963.45	$21.03	3	Jul 2021
Discover	$3,160.02	$162.48	10	Feb 2022
Mastercard	$5,303.57	$708.16	19	Nov 2022

The other method to pay down debt is the **avalanche method**. In this method, we pay off the card with the highest interest rate first. You will pay less interest this way, but as you will see in this example it's minimal.

1. Line up your credit cards from highest to lowest interest rate. Don't worry about the balance.
2. Figure out how much extra money you can pay in addition to the minimum payments.
3. Take this extra money and pay it to the card with the highest interest rate (the first one on your list.)
4. Pay the minimum balance on the cards with the lowest interest rates.
5. When the first card is paid off, take everything you paid to the first card and add it to the minimum payment of the card with the next highest interest rate.
6. Repeat this until all your credit cards are paid off.

Figure 13 is the timeline of payments for a person who has $500 a month to pay down this debt. In this case, Chase happens to have the highest interest rate and lowest balance.

Figure 13

Debt Avalanche- pay highest interest rate first							
#	Month	Chase	Mastercard	Discover	Snowball Amt.	Total Interest	Balance	Total Payments
1	May-21	$375.00	$75.00	$50.00	$355.00	$85.62	$8,545.00	$500.00
2	Jun-21	$375.00	$75.00	$50.00	$355.00	$80.75	$8,130.62	$500.00
3	Jul-21	$213.45	$236.55	$50.00	$375.00	$75.81	$7,711.37	$500.00
4	Aug-21	-	$450.00	$50.00	$375.00	$71.00	$7,284.60	$500.00
5	Sep-21	-	$450.00	$50.00	$375.00	$66.46	$6,855.60	$500.00
6	Oct-21	-	$450.00	$50.00	$375.00	$61.86	$6,422.06	$500.00
7	Nov-21	-	$450.00	$50.00	$375.00	$57.21	$5,983.92	$500.00
8	Dec-21	-	$450.00	$50.00	$375.00	$52.52	$5,541.13	$500.00
9	Jan-22	-	$450.00	$50.00	$375.00	$47.77	$5,093.65	$500.00
10	Feb-22	-	$450.00	$50.00	$375.00	$42.98	$4,641.42	$500.00
11	Mar-22	-	$450.00	$50.00	$375.00	$38.14	$4,184.40	$500.00
12	Apr-22	-	$450.00	$50.00	$375.00	$33.24	$3,722.54	$500.00
13	May-22	-	$450.00	$50.00	$375.00	$28.29	$3,255.78	$500.00
14	Jun-22	-	$129.08	$370.92	$450.00	$23.29	$2,784.07	$500.00
15	Jul-22	-	-	$500.00	$450.00	$19.02	$2,305.97	$500.00
16	Aug-22	-	-	$500.00	$450.00	$15.06	$1,824.99	$500.00
17	Sep-22	-	-	$500.00	$450.00	$11.06	$1,340.05	$500.00
18	Oct-22	-	-	$500.00	$450.00	$7.02	$851.11	$500.00
19	Nov-22	-	-	$358.13	$500.00	$2.95	$358.13	$358.13
20	Dec-22	-	-	-	$500.00	$0.00	$0.00	-
Total Interest Paid						$820.05		

Figure 14 illustrates that by following this method, the total principal and interest paid is $9,358. The total interest paid is $820 and percentage paid in interest is 8.76%. You would be debt free in 1.4 years or 17 months compared to the 8.2 years it would take if you paid only the minimum amount due.

Figure 14

Paying Only the Minimum Amount Due	
Total principal & interest:	$13,067
Total Interest:	$4,575
Percentage paid in interest:	35.01%
Years until debt free:	8.2 98 Month(s)
Debt free date:	Aug 2029

Your Selected Payoff Plan	
Total principal & interest:	$9,358
Total Interest:	$820
Percentage paid in interest:	8.76%
Years until debt free:	1.4 17 Month(s)
Debt free date:	Nov 2022

Account Payoff Details

Account	Total Payments	Projected Interest	Months to Payoff	Payoff Date
Chase	$963.45	$21.03	3	Jul 2021
Mastercard	$5,015.63	$417.02	14	Jun 2022
Discover	$3,379.05	$382.00	19	Nov 2022

As you can see by this example, you are debt free in the same amount of time, but you paid less interest using the avalanche method. It's not a huge difference. The amount saved will depend on your particular debts.

Both methods work if you stay consistent, but the snowball method may be better for you if you judge success by paying off cards entirely, even if it means paying a little more in interest over the long run to get out of debt. With both methods, if you slip up and miss a payment, get back on track as fast as you can. The more consistent you are with your payment the faster your snowball or avalanche will get you out of debt.

Once you pay off the debt, make sure you don't rack up those credit cards again. Only buy what you can afford to pay off in full each month, or better yet, pay cash and keep yourself out of debt once and for all. You'll be glad you did!

10. One of the Best Accounts in Which to Save Your Money

Most people use their bank account as the place to save their money. They either keep it in checking or savings or a combination of both. This wasn't a horrible idea when interest rates were higher, but these days, you are barely earning any interest in bank accounts. In today's world, the real purpose of these accounts is not to grow our money, but to give us the liquidity, use, and control over our money earned elsewhere.

What if I told you there was a better way to store money while also having it grow at a higher rate than what the bank offers? Would you want to know about that account, and more importantly, would you actually use it? If you answered yes, then you are in luck! Such an account does exist! Before I tell you what this account is, let me go over all of its features and how it works.

This mystery account has the same features as your savings account—liquidity, use, and control of your money—plus so much more. You can access your money at any time, use it for anything you want, and you own the account. One caveat is that not all the money you put in is available to you in the beginning of the contract. It takes a few years before the policy breaks even.

This account differs from your savings account in that it earns uninterrupted compound interest whether you use the money or not. I know you are thinking, "How can my account still earn interest if I take the money out? If I take money out of my savings account, isn't that money gone?" Actually, you aren't taking *your* money out of the account. You are using the financial institution's money and leaving your money inside the account to earn interest. This is known as collateralization. The financial institution loans you the money. Should you decide to not pay this loan back, which is usually an option, (not to mention another benefit of setting up an account and borrowing in this manner) the institution will recover what it is owed from the account used to secure the loan repayment. I recommend that you be a good banker and pay back the money you owe with interest so you can continue to build wealth.

One way the institution is paid back is it comes off of the death benefit. When you repay the debt this way, you are really borrowing from your dead self. Say the death benefit is $500,000, and you have a loan for $50,000. Then you die. Your beneficiary would get $450,000 instead of the $500,000 because that $50,000 would go toward repaying the loan.

In retirement, you won't have to pay the loans back as long as they are structured properly, and for that, you would need the advice of a good financial planner. If you allow the policy to lapse because let's say you took out too much money, you may have a taxable event.

The next features of this account are tax-deferred growth and tax-free distribution. Tax-deferred means you are not paying taxes each year on your money and the growth of your money. You will not receive a 1099 tax statement at the end of each year as you do with your savings account or investment account. Savings accounts and investment accounts funded with pre-tax money are considered taxable accounts, which is why you get a 1099 statement from the earnings on these accounts.

What is even better than tax-deferred? Yes, you guessed it: tax-free! When you take money from this account, it comes out tax-free in the form of a loan or withdrawals up to the amount of money that you paid into the account, which is also known as basis. This account also earns dividends in addition to what you contribute to the account.

What are you earning on your savings account? .001%? Would you like an account that has a competitive long-term rate of return? This account does. It earns uninterrupted compound interest. The interest rate of the dividend is 4% to 4.7%. Remember, this is tax free, and dividends are not guaranteed. However, I work with companies who have consistently paid dividends.

Another benefit of this account is that it allows for high contributions. You get to decide how much you want to contribute, and the account is designed to accommodate that number. Contributions are not limited like they are in a 401(k), Roth IRA, or traditional IRA. There are no income limitations as there are with a Roth IRA. This is a great feature for high income earners who are ineligible to contribute to a Roth IRA. The account can be structured in a way that allows you to contribute as much as you want; subject to insurability and the insurance company's limit based on your age and income.

During the pandemic, we have seen the benefit of this next feature: a guaranteed loan option. Some of my clients used this account while they were waiting for their stimulus checks and/or PPP loans. You simply pick up the phone and call the company, and within a couple of days, the money is in your bank account. No long application or proof of income is required to borrow money from this account. No waiting to find out if your loan was approved. And YOU get to decide when you pay back the loan.

People without this account had to wait for their unemployment checks, which were often delayed. Other people tried to get a home equity line of credit or loan, but during this pandemic, many banks like Wells Fargo stopped issuing home equity loans. Even if they hadn't stopped, if you lost your job and tried to refinance or get a home equity loan, you would most likely be denied because banks want to see that you have the ability to repay the loan. Makes you wonder why are you in such a rush to pay off your house if that would be the place you go to get money during an emergency. You also have to pay the financial institution to get at that money. If all your money is tied up in your house, your only options to get at that money would be to sell your house or arrange for a new line of credit, which might cost additional fees and closing costs that could have been avoided if you did not rush to pay off this debt. Yes, we are in a seller's market as I write this. You will get a great price for your house, but where are you going to live? The other houses on the market will also have a higher price tag.

If you can't get your money from your house, where else can you get it? Some people have it in the stock market. But if you have all your money in the stock market, you wouldn't want to take it out when the market is doing well because you wouldn't want to miss out on the gains. You also wouldn't want to take out your money in a down market because your money would have locked in your losses. More on this in a later chapter.

2020 was certainly the year of clear vision. What you have been led to believe about money by the so-called experts isn't the whole truth. Paying off your house and putting all your money in the market isn't a complete financial plan. This pandemic has certainly taught us that access to capital is a critical feature that is often overlooked. Lucky for you, this book gives you the strategies you need to build your wealth.

Just like a savings account, the money in this mystery account is safe. In fact, the guaranteed cash value of the account is not limited, unlike the FDIC limit of $250,000 that you probably have on your checking or savings account. The amount of money you contribute and the interest you earn is guaranteed and not subject to market volatility or losses. The only way you would lose money is if you cancelled the account prematurely or if the loan balance lapsed the policy. Remember, this is a long-term strategy. Discipline is key when it comes to saving continuously. Money in this account is also liquid.

How great would it be to have a loan that you pay back on your terms and potentially not even during your lifetime? That is one of the greatest features of this account. You determine the payback schedule, which provides you with great flexibility. As mentioned above, your loan doesn't have to be paid back, but I highly advise you do so during your accumulation years when possible (but review chapter nine on higher interest rate debts, which should be paid off before paying off the loans secured by this account). You want to pay back what you took out with interest as this is how you build wealth, but you also want to do so with a smart plan in mind.

Some additional benefits of this account are creditor protection, depending on the state you live in, and disability protection. If you are no longer able to make contributions to this account and you add disability protection, the institution will pay the contributions for you. You can't get that in a savings account! Also, when you die, the account will pay you a death benefit. The death benefit is always "at least" the value of the cash account and almost always more. The death benefit is also tax-free.

All these benefits sound great, but what is this mystery account we are talking about? The answer is permanent cash value life insurance. The benefits discussed above are specific to whole life insurance. Now, before you go ahead and close this book, please take a deep breath and put aside everything you have heard before about life insurance. The IRS tax code has changed in many ways, and the product I am talking about is relatively new. So, I suggest going back to the chapter on releasing money blocks and walking through the exercise if this is a block for you.

This is not just any type of permanent cash value life insurance. It has to be structured properly in a way that is designed to maximize the cash value and minimize the death benefit. The IRS has also set rules on exactly how much can be contributed to this account without it becoming taxable, so it is important to work with a licensed agent and preferably someone who also has the CFP® designation when setting this up.

Essentially, you pay more premium than is required to maintain the death benefit for the policy. This is known as overfunding a policy. Many agents aren't aware that you can do this with life insurance, so you will want to find an agent who knows how to design these policies for your benefit. Agents are paid a commission based on death benefits. The higher the death benefit the higher their commission, so they might want to sell you a policy with the highest possible death benefit. Even though it means being paid less, I want to do the opposite because I want to help you.

If you are using a whole life policy, you can choose how long you want to pay premiums. There are policies that are paid up after ten or twenty years, at age sixty-five, and even those where you can pay until you are 100 years old and still receive tax-deferred growth and tax-free withdrawals! Even if you have a policy that can be paid to age 100, you don't have to pay the premiums because at some point, the dividends will be large enough to pay the premiums for you. But for those clients seeking the ability to continue the tax-deferred growth, they can choose to continue making these payments. There are other options as well if you don't want to pay the premium. When you see the cash value going up by more than the premium payment, you may not want to ever stop paying the premium. You have options on what you want to do with the policy.

11. Who Should and Shouldn't Have an Overfunded Life Insurance Policy?

Although this type of policy is a great addition to your financial plan, an overfunded life insurance policy is not for everyone. Let's explore why an overfunded policy might *not* work for you and some alternative options you can choose instead.

Age and Health

The cost of insurance increases with age. The younger and healthier you are the lower your cost of insurance will be, so you'll want to get a good health rating, otherwise this strategy wouldn't be the best way for you to save. If you are only looking for a death benefit, an overfunded permanent cash value policy like this would be too costly and an inefficient use of your money. A different policy design would better suit your needs, and you should not buy one just so an agent can get paid his or her commission.

Not Enough Saved

In order to really see the benefits, you want to be able to pay between $5,000 and $10,000 a year into this policy. Ideally, you should save $10,000 because the more you put into the policy the more it grows. If you don't have that amount saved up, you may want to get a term policy from a good company (not necessarily the cheapest you can find), and make sure that policy is convertible to a strong whole life or indexed universal life policy in the future. This way, you lock in your health rating and insurability, and you will not have to go through underwriting when you are able to afford the permanent policy.

You Want to See Immediate Results

This is a long-term strategy, as in ten to twenty years and longer. This is when you'll really see the power of compounding and cash value. Discipline is key here. If you are not used to saving on a monthly, quarterly, or annual basis or willing to commit to a long-term savings strategy, this is not for you. You will probably see cash value in the first year of the policy. but it won't be equal to what you paid in premiums. Remember, this is life insurance after all. In traditionally funded policies where you only pay the premium required to support the death benefit, you won't see cash value until the third year. The breakeven point on overfunded policies is usually about seven to ten years. Then, the cash value is more than the premiums you paid. The longer you own the policy the more cash compounds exponentially. It's the time value of money and the uninterrupted compounding effect. When you get to the point where you use this policy for retirement income, you will most likely pull out more income than you have paid into the policy in premiums according to the whole life illustrations I've run. This is not to say that you have to wait to start borrowing money against your policy. You can do that as soon as there is cash value. If you aren't concerned with accessing the cash value, again, this might not be right for you.

Who *Should* Have an Overfunded Policy?

This strategy works for someone who is looking to maximize their cash flow by using a policy like this to finance major capital purchases, such as cars and business equipment. For someone who is looking to maximize their retirement cash flow, minimize taxes in retirement, and have a plan for market volatility, this is a piece that should definitely be included in your financial plan. I will show you how to make major capital purchases and how retirement plans work in the upcoming chapters.

Other Policy Options

If you are strictly looking for tax-free retirement income, you will want a policy design that gives you a larger income stream in retirement. I like whole life insurance because of the guarantees it provides, and the companies that I write pay dividends. If you want the potential to have higher cash value, then I like index universal life (IUL) insurance policies.

Let's talk about how an IUL policy works. If you are using an IUL policy, there are no dividends. It earns interest based on the index you select (i.e. the S&P 500 index). Each company has different indexing strategies. Some are capped while other strategies are uncapped. Here's an example. Say your cash value is in the S&P 500 index, and it earns 15%. If your policy states that the policy is capped at 10%, then 10% would be credited to your cash account. If the index earns 4%, you will get 4% credited to your cash value account. If the policy is uncapped, you would get a credit for whatever percentage the index earns. I won't get into the nitty-gritty here. I just want to make you aware of another permanent life policy you could choose to overfund.

If you are looking for protection and a lot of coverage, term insurance or a blend of term insurance and permanent insurance may be right for you. If you are looking for a low-cost permanent death benefit to transfer your wealth to the next generation, then a guaranteed universal life or low-cost universal life policy may be right for you.

Given all of the options, you definitely want to make sure you are dealing with someone who is willing to take the time to get to know you and your individual situation and who is also familiar with how to structure insurance properly for your needs. If you have someone, great! If not, you can reach out to me, and I'd be happy to help.

12. How to Use Your Overfunded Life Insurance Policy as Your Bank

Just to be clear, an overfunded life insurance policy is in addition to your banking accounts at your bank. You cannot replace your bank entirely, but a properly designed policy is a great place for your long-term savings. Contrary to popular belief, you finance everything you buy. Even if you pay cash, you are giving up the interest you could have earned on your money. Banks don't lose interest, and neither should you.

Let's look at how banks work. Banks need our money to be profitable. We walk into a bank, give them our hard-earned money, and these days, they pay us .001% interest. I remember back in 2005 I had a money market paying 4%. They also used to give free gifts like toasters. I think now you get a water bottle, if that. Now that they have our money, they can lend out nine times this amount. This is called fractional reserve banking.

Fractional reserve banking boils down to this: let's say you found a really nice bank and they are going to give you 2% on your money. They will turn around and loan that to someone for a personal loan at 10%, a car loan at 4%, a fifteen-year mortgage at 2.5%, etc. Banks are one of the most profitable businesses in the world, which is why you see one at almost every corner. They tell you to leave your money with them for as long as possible, but they don't follow that advice—they lend it out as soon as possible!

When you structure your overfunded policy correctly, you are creating your own bank. You put your money in the policy through premiums which are equivalent to deposits in your bank account. You want most of the premium going to the paid-up additions rider (PUA), a savings component which allows you to pay more premiums than required to keep the policy enforced. And you want the minimum death benefit for the amount of premiums you are paying into the policy, thereby lowering the cost of insurance.

The policy earns interest and dividends. Your money is earning uninterrupted compound interest. When you take money out of the policy via a loan, you aren't borrowing your money. You are borrowing the insurance company's money, so your money continues to grow. Again, you want to make sure you are working with a good insurance company that offers non-direct recognition. Non-direct recognition means the insurance company does NOT reduce the amount of your account on which you are paid a dividend when there is a loan against the policy. Instead, they treat the loan separately and continue to pay a dividend on the account value without any reduction for the loan amount accounted for elsewhere. In other words, they don't "recognize" that you took out a loan.

That is the gist of how to set up this policy when using it as your "bank." There's a lot more detail to it, which is why working with a good financial planner or insurance agent who knows the ins and outs of this policy design is so important.

Now that you've set up your insurance policy "bank," how do you use it? Many people use this strategy to purchase cars, pay for weddings, college, etc. For example, if using this strategy to buy a car, you first need to pay the premiums and wait until there is enough cash value so you can take a loan to go and buy your car. Remember, this is a long-term strategy, so you won't see immediate results. You won't be able to go buy a car immediately after opening an account, but you could use this strategy to buy your second car in five years.

So, let's say you are paying $12,000 a year in premiums, and in five years, you have roughly $51,000 of cash value. You want to buy a car that costs $25,000, so you take a loan against the policy for $25,000. Then, to pay the loan back, you plan to make payments of $5,000 to $6,000 a year for the next five years, plus some amount of interest (which you don't mind paying because you are paying it to yourself in your own bank). You are also paying the premiums, so it's $17,000 to $18,000 out of pocket for those five years. Rather than paying the bank $6,000 a year, you are putting the $6,000 a year into *your* bank.

You can do this every time you purchase a car. If you miss a payment with a traditional car loan, they can repossess your car. However, with a loan from the insurance company, you can skip a payment if you'd like. Again, I caution against this as you want to be a good banker, but in case of an emergency, you have that flexibility. Another benefit of purchasing your car this way is that, even though you have a loan against the policy, your cash value is still earning uninterrupted compounding interest.

Remember, this strategy only works for people who are savers as you are still going to pay those premiums. Think of the premiums as what you would throw into a savings account each year until you read this book.

Here's a personal story of what can happen if you are undisciplined in paying your life insurance policy. I took a loan for almost the maximum allowed by my policy, and I never paid it back. It was for something stupid, and I told myself I would just open a new policy and pay double the premium I was for the first policy. But you can't make up lost time. Remember the time value of money. We are all human, and when it's our own money, we can make poor choices. I did things I would never advise my clients to do.

I ended up canceling that new policy as well. The problem was discipline. I didn't have the discipline to pay the loan back on my policy, and I was stubborn. Here is where I cut off my nose to spite my face. I had a rental property that had about $80,000 of equity, and I owed $17,000 on my car. I attempted to refinance my house for a lower interest rate and to use some of the cash to pay off the loan and invest the rest. I am not recommending anyone do this. I do not advise people to take out money from their house to invest. It is okay to refinance if it will get you out of debt and increase your cash flow. You should also make sure you won't get yourself back into debt. Otherwise, this is not for you and you will likely only worsen your financial situation.

I worked out the numbers, and my rental property would still be profitable even with the cash out refinance. I would have freed up an extra $550 a month in cash flow. Everything looked great on paper until the underwriter reviewed my financials. As a business owner, I write off everything I possibly can. That was my first mistake. To anyone who is reading this that owns a business, make sure you have everything you want (like a house) before you show minimal income.

The second issue the underwriter saw was the rent I paid for my apartment was too high compared to the income I was showing. Really? Didn't they realize since I pay all my bills on time and my credit score is 835, I would have an easier time paying all of my bills with having an even better cash flow position? How could I live and pay my bills if I didn't make enough to support myself?

All my money was trapped in my house, and there was nothing I could do about it. Had I kept my first insurance policy in place and paid the loan back, I would have at least been able to free up the $550 a month of cash flow. Yes, I would have paid the policy loan back and used the dividends to help reduce the loan, but it would have been on my terms. I could decide how much I wanted to pay back and when I wanted to pay it back.

The moral of this story is I should have kept my policy. The bank required a ton of documentation and still turned me down. But if I still had my policy, I would just have to call the insurance company, and I would have had my money within twenty-four hours. Having an overfunded option gives you liquidity, use, control, and freedom with your money.

13. How to Pay for College without Going Broke

Paying for college is one of the largest expenses you will have in your life. A four-year degree can cost as much as $250,000. Parents of multiple children probably worry constantly about this expense. The good news is that, through proper planning, you can pay for college without going broke.

There are many types of accounts where you can save money for educational purposes in a tax-favored manner. The 529 plan is one of the most popular types of account I see.

If this plan is used specifically for college, the money in the account is nontaxable, and it also grows tax-free within the account. While those are both wonderful benefits, there are several drawbacks to using a 529 plan for college.

In some cases, it could actually hurt you if the money is not used for college. If you choose to use it for something else, all the earnings on this account will be taxed at your current bracket, and a 10% penalty might be imposed by the IRS. 529 plans are usually invested in mutual funds, so they are also subject to market fluctuations. This could be a positive or a negative. For example, if you've lost money in a bad market and are ready to use the money for college, you may not have as much money in the account as you would if you took it out in an up market.

A colleague of mine experienced a different type of drawback to owning a 529 plan. His son received a full scholarship, but he was required to spend everything in his 529 before receiving those scholarship funds. Clearly, there are pros and cons to setting up a 529 plan. You should consider these factors and plan carefully before jumping in just because it worked out for someone else!

I would like to introduce another option to be considered, which in my opinion, is one of the most underutilized and misunderstood asset classes out there: cash value life insurance. Today's cash value life insurance has many new and innovative living benefits, along with a tax efficient strategy to accumulate money that can be used to fund college or your retirement.

The cash value grows tax-deferred, and if structured and utilized properly, the cash can be taken out tax-free from the policy. Life insurance is also one of the few assets not counted on the FAFSA form. Thus, a parent funding a life insurance policy instead of a bank account may show fewer assets available to pay for college, and their child may receive more federal student aid accordingly.

When choosing a college, you shouldn't automatically assume that State schools are going to be cheaper. In many cases, a private school can actually cost less than a state school given the same financial need and curriculum of the student. How can this be? Private schools usually have large endowments and fewer students, meaning they can offer more aid regardless of the parent's income and assets.

The sooner you start planning and saving for your child the better. If your child is already in high school, it's not too late to save. You can design a life insurance policy to lower your Effective Family Contribution (EFC), which is what colleges require you to pay if you were to attend their school. So, a lower number would potentially get you more financial aid.

14. Reasons You Should Have a Mortgage

There are four reasons to have a mortgage:
1. You don't have enough cash to pay for the house
2. The tax deduction
3. The potential spread between what your money can earn and the cost to borrow money
4. To have liquidity, use, and control of your money—the most important reason!

If you don't have enough money to pay cash for a house, it's obvious you need to have a mortgage. Let's talk about inflation for a minute. The most valuable dollars you have are the ones you have in your pocket today. In today's dollars, a $2,000 monthly mortgage payment with 3% inflation will feel like $823.97 thirty years from now. Your money will never be worth more than it is today. Wouldn't you rather hold on to your most valuable dollars?

What if you did have the money and wanted to pay cash for a house that costs $300,000? Rather than paying cash for the house, if you kept your money and earned 6% on your $300,000 for thirty years, that would equal $1,806,773. If you paid cash for your house, this is your opportunity cost—your loss of potential gain—because now the money is in your house and earning 0%. I'll come back to that in a minute. If you took out a thirty-year mortgage at 4.5%, your monthly payment would be $1,520. The total cost to own this home (principal, interest, and opportunity) is $1,526,919. It makes sense to have a mortgage because your money can earn more than the mortgage is costing you.

Now, let's factor in the tax deduction. If you are in the 30% tax bracket, the net cost to borrow is 3.15%, and the total cost to have the mortgage is $1,295,031. Not everyone can claim the mortgage deduction, so be sure to check with your tax adviser. With a thirty-year mortgage, you get more of a deduction in the first fifteen years than you would if you had a fifteen-year mortgage. As you can see, the potential spread and tax deduction make it a wise decision to have a mortgage. Of course, there are reasons to rent instead (i.e. you won't have to pay property taxes), so always make sure to look at the pros and cons when making the decision.

Finally, let's talk about control. Back to what I said earlier, the money (equity) in your house earns 0%. Equity is not determined by how much money you have in the house but by appreciation, which is the increase of the property's value over time. Why would you want to tie up your money in something that earns 0%? The only way to get this money is to borrow against or sell your house. What if you should lose your job, become disabled, or your home is destroyed by a natural disaster? If the money is in your house, you will be unable to get at the equity. If you have your money in an account that you can readily access, you can weather the storm until your circumstances change. At some point, your side fund is going to be enough to pay off your house if you choose to do so.

Knowing what you know now, would you want to give up your most valuable dollars? I wouldn't.

15. In Case Of A Natural Disaster, Should You (Or Your Bank) Own Your House?

What comes to mind when you think of protecting your house from natural disasters such as hurricanes or floods? Most would rely on their homeowner's insurance or flood insurance to keep them comfortable; that's what we pay for. If your house was destroyed by a natural disaster, your insurance company would indeed pay to have it repaired, and they would provide you with living assistance while progress is made. But keep in mind everyone else in your community who also lost their house will be in the same boat as you, which makes finding a nearby, available hotel room within your benefit's budget or limited per diem amount very difficult. The living assistance you'd receive is likely to translate into a standard room at a Motel 6 where they can find space.

In theory, this cushion is a comfort, but combined with the sudden, overwhelming demand for contractors, the repairs are likely to stretch over months, deflating your initial appreciation and confidence in your preparedness. It would be awhile before you were back to living in your house and cooking your own meals. Unless you can afford to rent one of the homes left on the market or walk away from the shell of your home, the coverage of home and flood insurance simply doesn't measure up.

Facing this discomfort as a family in the wake of disaster can lead to emotional financial decisions, which we learned in a previous chapter can be detrimental. For example, some people may choose to tap into retirement accounts to boost daily quality of life and cover the basics not provided for by insurance so they can try to recapture a sense of peace. Protecting your home's true value demands more than homeowner's insurance so it doesn't devastate your overall financial position.

Most people feel they are more secure by having their house paid off. I believe you are more secure by having a mortgage *and* having your money in cash value life insurance. This gives you access, liquidity, and control of your money when you need it. So, let's look at three emotional and financial reasons to have a mortgage and life insurance combination.

In scenario one, you lose your job. So, you go to the bank and try to get some money out of the house. Your house is worth $500,000, and you owe $100,000 on your mortgage, which means you have access to $400,000. Not so fast! Since you don't have a job, the bank is going to be worried about how you are going to pay them back, and they won't give you a loan. All your money is tied up in your house. If you had your money in a life insurance policy, you wouldn't need permission to access it.

In scenario two, you become disabled. Even if you have disability insurance and you have a big mortgage, as long as you have access to capital inside of cash value life insurance policy, you are in a better financial position than having no mortgage and no access to capital. This enables you to deal with your new circumstances.

In scenario three, we're back to your house that is now destroyed. Because you have cash value, you can get out of the motel and go rent an apartment until your house is rebuilt. The bank will be happy to give you a loan because you can use your life insurance as collateral. You have the option to walk away from the house and deal with a bad credit score for seven years, which I am not recommending, but in certain instances, this may be a good option depending on your individual situation. Properly funded life insurance should be a protection strategy that homeowners use.

You can always get in a position of having your house paid off, but it is difficult to get a loan on your house when you really need it. The number one reason people want to have their house paid off is to eliminate the monthly payment. When you have your money in a safe place like a life insurance policy rather than in your house, eliminating the monthly payment can be accomplished without sacrificing protection. Do you want to own your house if it was struck by a natural disaster or do you want the bank to?

16. The Truth about Qualified Retirement Plans

Retirement plans, for example a qualified plan like your 401(k), does two things: (i) they defer the payment of taxes (but they do not necessarily save taxes) and (ii) they defer the tax calculation.

Let me illustrate how qualified plans actually work. Say you borrowed $10,000 from me. Before you cash that check you'll ask me when you have to pay it back and how much interest I'm going to charge. If I told you I don't need the money now, but there will come a time in the future when I do at which point, I'll calculate how much I need and what interest you will have to pay me, are you going to cash that check? No way! But that is exactly what the government is doing with qualified plans.

There is value in putting money in a 401(k) up to the match, but not a penny more. Most people think that by retirement age, they will be in a lower tax bracket. Do you really want to reduce your standard of living, or do you just want to pay the least amount of taxes? You probably want to pay the least amount of taxes when you retire, but this isn't always the case. If you are in a lower bracket, then you will be better served by deferring the taxes. Many financial planners, me included, believe tax rates are going up, or the decision makers in Congress will lower the top thresholds, resulting in the government being able to collect more money. Based on this, I do not believe you can realistically expect to be a lower tax bracket.

The national debt is $27 trillion and rising, and we haven't even seen the biggest wave of Baby Boomers retiring yet. 70% of baby boomers are set to retire between 2022 and 2030. Guess where most Americans have their wealth? Yes, in their retirement plans. Who do you think the government is going to go after—the people who have money or the people who don't? Based on this, the odds that you will be in a lower tax bracket are very low.

Over their lifetime, people drive to work every day in cars that were most likely financed and replaced every three to five years. They overfund their retirement plans at work so they could get a tax deduction, and they hurry up to pay off their house as quickly as possible with the hope that then they can really start saving for retirement. In doing this, they received a deduction through their 401(k) plan only to lose a deduction in their home mortgage. Qualified plans have many inefficiencies.

Whose retirement dream are you chasing—yours or Uncle Sam's? Let's look at an example of what happens when you're ready to use the money in your 401(k) for retirement. These numbers are rounded for ease of understanding.

Every year for thirty-five years, you put $6,000 in your 401(k), which equals $210,000 total contribution. Let's assume you're in a 32% tax bracket. It appears your tax savings is $2,000 a year, which is $6,000 x 32%. After thirty-five years, you would have $70,000 in total "tax savings." Let's assume you've earned 7.5% interest over thirty-five years. Now your balance after those thirty-five years grew to $1,000,000. You're afraid to spend principal because you don't want to run out of money so you only withdraw the interest.

Figure 15 illustrates this example.

Figure 15

	$ 1,000,000	
X	7.50%	
	$75,000	Retirement Income
X	32%	Tax Rate
$	24,000	Annual Tax
$	51,000	Net Spendable Income
$	**70,000**	Tax Savings for 35yrs
$	**72,000**	Taxes in 1st 3 Retirement Years
$	**480,000**	Total tax by year 20

In this example, the person "saved" $70,000 in taxes only to later pay $480,000 in taxes over a twenty-year retirement. By the third year, you've already paid more in taxes than you saved over thirty-five years. This is if tax rates stay the same, which I don't believe will happen.

The good news is you have choices. There are alternatives to qualified plans to save money and vehicles that also let you enjoy tax-free treatment. If you are under the income limit for contributing to a Roth IRA, you can put the maximum allowable contribution into that account. As of 2021, if you are fifty years or older, you can contribute up to $7,000. If your modified adjusted gross income is under $208,000 for married couples and under $140,000 for a single person, you can contribute to a Roth IRA. For those people above the income limits to be able to contribute to a Roth IRA, inquire if your 401(k) has a Roth option. You might be able to direct a portion of your contribution to that.

Another option is to do a Roth conversion. This is good to do in a market downturn. 2020 was a great year to do this if your income was reduced due to COVID-19. A financial professional will be able to help you evaluate if a Roth conversion makes sense for you based on your particular financial situation. If you do this, you will want to make sure you have other money to pay the taxes and not take it from the IRA that you are converting. If you are receiving Social Security or are on

Medicare, you also want to take into account if this will cause your Social Security payments to be taxed at a higher rate and cause your Medicare premiums to increase.

A Roth conversion is when you move money from your tax-deductible traditional IRA to a non-deductible Roth IRA. You pay tax on the funds when you move them to the Roth IRA, but if you have held the account for five years, you don't pay tax when you withdraw those funds or the gains from them in retirement. If drawn before retirement and depending on the reason for withdrawal, a portion of the withdrawal may be taxable. You can always get your contributions back tax-free. There are all kinds of rules for how and when you can withdraw your money from a Roth IRA, so please check with your financial planner before doing so.

I'm not saying your retirement plan is bad, and that you shouldn't contribute to it. I just wanted to give you the whole story about how to save for your retirement. There is another vehicle that you would be wise to include in your retirement plan. We will take a deeper look into that in the next chapter.

17. Using Life Insurance to Supplement Your Retirement

Life insurance is a great way to supplement your retirement income. I believe you need to have two buckets of money in retirement: a risk bucket and a safe money bucket. Let's talk about the safe bucket. Whole life insurance is similar to a Roth IRA, but it's even better because you don't have the income or contribution limit restriction. Both allow for after-tax contributions, tax-deferred growth, and tax-free distribution. By now, you are familiar with all other benefits of whole life insurance described in an earlier chapter.

We also reviewed the contribution limits of a Roth IRA. If you want to contribute more than $6,000 a year, your only other option that has tax-free benefits is overfunded life insurance, whole life, or indexed universal life (IUL). Life insurance policies can be structured to accept more than this, which can help if you are trying to catch up and build savings before you retire. This is considered your safe bucket because whole life has guaranteed cash values and is not subject to market volatility like a Roth IRA would be if it is invested in the market. You have access to your cash value should you need it before retirement without penalty. The Roth IRA has restrictions on when and how you can get you money out.

Another way to use life insurance in your retirement plan is as a volatility buffer. Going back to your buckets, any money invested in the market is your risk bucket. You need to have both buckets to use life insurance as a volatility buffer. When you are retired, you don't want to take money out of your retirement account when the market is down because your account will run out sooner. If you have life insurance as part of your retirement, you can take the money you would have taken from your retirement account out of your life insurance the year following when the market was down.

To illustrate a retirement scenario, let's use a hypothetical example provided by the Ohio National Financial Service. Katherine is a forty-five-year-old attorney, and when she retires at sixty-five she will have $1.5 million in her retirement account. Her plan is to withdraw $100,000 a year for income. Conservatively, we will project a 5% average annual return. After ten years, Katherine still has more than $1.12 million. Figure 16 illustrates this example.

Figure 16

Katherine's Age	Account Balance on Jan. 1	Withdrawal on Jan. 1	Balance After Withdrawal	Average Annual Return	End of Year Account Balance	
65	$1,500,000	$100,000	$1,400,000	5.00%	$1,470,000	Note the consistent 5% average annual return each year.
66	$1,470,000	$100,000	$1,370,000	5.00%	$1,438,500	
67	$1,438,500	$100,000	$1,338,500	5.00%	$1,405,425	
68	$1,405,425	$100,000	$1,305,425	5.00%	$1,370,696	
69	$1,370,696	$100,000	$1,270,696	5.00%	$1,334,231	
70	$1,334,231	$100,000	$1,234,231	5.00%	$1,295,942	
71	$1,295,942	$100,000	$1,195,942	5.00%	$1,255,739	More than $1.12 million still available after 10 years of withdrawals.
72	$1,255,739	$100,000	$1,155,739	5.00%	$1,213,526	
73	$1,213,526	$100,000	$1,113,526	5.00%	$1,169,202	
74	$1,169,202	$100,000	$1,069,202	5.00%	$1,122,662	
				5.00% Annual Average Return		

Note: Ohio National Financial Services. *Life Insurance Retirement Supplement: Manage your retirement income with life insurance*, 2020, p. 3.

This is unrealistic because markets don't return 5% every year. In the real world, the stock market returns are different every year. Let's look at the actual returns of the S&P 500 between 2002 and 2011 and include them in Katherine's example. This is illustrated in Figure 17.

Figure 17

Katherine's Age	Year	Account Balance on Jan. 1	Withdrawal on Jan. 1	Balance After Withdrawal	S&P 500 Returns	End of Year Account Balance	
65	2002	$1,500,000	$100,000	$1,400,000	-22.10%	$1,090,600	The S&P 500® is a commonly used indicator of overall U.S. stock market performance.
66	2003	$1,090,600	$100,000	$990,600	28.68%	$1,274,704	
67	2004	$1,274,704	$100,000	$1,174,704	10.88%	$1,302,512	
68	2005	$1,302,512	$100,000	$1,202,513	4.91%	$1,261,556	
69	2006	$1,261,556	$100,000	$1,161,556	15.79%	$1,344,966	**More than $354,000 less** than previous example. Katherine may not be able to withdraw $100,000 again due to her low account value.
70	2007	$1,344,966	$100,000	$1,244,966	5.49%	$1,313,315	
71	2008	$1,313,315	$100,000	$1,213,315	-37.00%	$764,388	
72	2009	$764,388	$100,000	$664,388	26.46%	$840,185	
73	2010	$840,185	$100,000	$740,185	15.10%	$851,953	
74	2011	$851,953	$100,000	$751,953	2.10%	**$767,744**	
					5.03% Annual Average Return		

Note: Ohio National Financial Services. *Life Insurance Retirement Supplement: Manage your retirement income with life insurance*, 2020, p. 4.

While the average annual rate is close to 5%, there is a difference of more than $354,000 in Katherine's final account balance. If she wants her income to last for the rest of her life, she needs to carefully decide if she should draw another $100,000 at the end of ten years.

What if there was a way she could adjust her income withdrawals and "manage" these negative returns? Luckily, she can do this if she doesn't take a withdrawal from her retirement account in the following year after a market downturn. Figure 18 shows how her account could be $319,795 higher than in the prior example at the end of ten years if she did not take the $100,000 withdrawals in any year following a market downturn.

Figure 18

No withdrawals the year after a negative market.

Katherine's Age	Year	Account Balance on Jan. 1	Withdrawal on Jan. 1	Balance After Withdrawal	S&P 500 Returns	End of Year Account Balance
65	2002	$1,500,000	$100,000	$1,400,000	-22.10%	$1,090,600
66	2003	$1,090,600	$0	$1,090,600	28.68%	$1,403,384
67	2004	$1,403,384	$100,000	$1,303,384	10.88%	$1,445,192
68	2005	$1,445,192	$100,000	$1,345,192	4.91%	$1,411,241
69	2006	$1,411,241	$100,000	$1,311,241	15.79%	$1,518,286
70	2007	$1,518,286	$100,000	$1,418,286	5.49%	$1,496,150
71	2008	$1,496,150	$100,000	$1,396,150	-37.00%	$879,575
72	2009	$879,575	$0	$879,575	26.46%	$1,112,311
73	2010	$1,112,311	$100,000	$1,012,311	15.10%	$1,165,170
74	2011	$1,165,170	$100,000	$1,065,170	2.10%	$1,087,539

$319,795 more than the previous example.

Note: Ohio National Financial Services. *Life Insurance Retirement Supplement: Manage your retirement income with life insurance*, 2020, p. 5.

You are probably thinking, "That makes sense, but where is she going to get the $100,000 of income she needs to live on?" That's exactly where life insurance comes in. Instead of taking the $100,000 out of her retirement account the two years following the down markets, she takes it out of her insurance policy for those two years. Let's look at Figure 19 for a whole life policy example. She receives the best health rating class and pays out-of-pocket premiums of $19,692 to age sixty-five. Policy values (i.e. dividends and cash value) are illustrated to cover premiums from age sixty-six to 100.

Figure 19

	End of Year Age	Policy Premium	Policy Loan Amount	Cash Value Increase (Current)*	Total Cash Surrender Value (Current)*	Total Death Benefit (Current)*
Annual premium of $19,692.	46	$19,692	–	$0	$0	$1,118,308
Income tax-free policy loans at ages 66 and 72 to balance negative returns on retirement savings.	47	$19,692	–	$948	$948	$1,164,281
	48	$19,692	–	$14,581	$15,529	$1,149,576
	65	$19,692	–	$46,067	**$517,999**	$1,188,483
	66	$19,692	–	$27,779	$545,778	$1,186,758
Policy values cover premiums from age 66 to 100.	67	$19,692	$100,000	-$76,194	$469,583	$1,180,968
	72	$19,692	–	$30,641	$608,074	$1,167,017
	73	$19,692	$100,000	-$72,413	$535,661	$1,163,330
	74	$19,692	–	$28,952	$564,613	$1,160,787
	75	$19,692	–	$30,310	$594,923	**$1,159,392**

Current cash value grows to over $510,000 at age 65

A current death benefit of over $1.1 million at age 75.

* Using current dividend scale. Values shown use end-of-year ages and projected based on the current dividend scale and not guaranteed. For guaranteed values and other important information, see the sample illustration at the back of this brochure.

Note: The example assumes a $100,000 loan. However, because loans from certain life insurance policies are currently income tax-free under certain conditions, she would be able to take less money and still have the same after-tax cash flow as if she had taken the money from her retirement accounts.

[1] Dividends are not guaranteed.

[2] Loans, and withdrawals, if taken, will reduce the death benefit. Loans and withdrawals from life insurance policies that are classified as modified endowment contracts may be subject to tax at the time that the loan or withdrawal is taken and, if taken prior to age 59½, a 10% federal tax penalty may apply. If tax-free loans are taken and the policy lapses, a taxable event may occur.

Note: Ohio National Financial Services. *Life Insurance Retirement Supplement: Manage your retirement income with life insurance*, 2020, p. 7.

It's a very smart move to have investments and life insurance as part of your retirement plan, not only for the volatility buffer but for the long-term care benefits and the tax-free death benefit. If you have a long-term care need, you can access a portion of the death benefit to cover that need. Some people are afraid to spend their money because they want to leave money to their kids or grandkids. Having life insurance gives you a "permission slip" to do so.

18. Case Studies

You may be wondering how all this applies to you and your particular situation. I will go over some scenarios with clients who I have helped. Their names are changed to protect their identities.

Monica

I received a call on a Monday morning from Monica, a long-time client of mine. She called me in a panic because she was worried about running out of money. She did the math over the weekend and came to the conclusion that if she kept withdrawing money from her account at her current rate, it wouldn't last long enough. I confirmed this, saying she would run out of money if she was trying to handle her money on her own. But that was not the case because she had me. We already had a strategy in place so she would have an income that would last her to the day she died.

She had an annuity which provided income for life. In her particular annuity, if the index earned interest every year, she would automatically get an increase in her income. This new income threshold is then locked in. She could potentially have a guaranteed increasing income stream.

When I told her she might be able to withdraw even more money than she currently was and still not run out of money, she was thrilled. She felt great knowing she was going to have an income that she could not outlive and that would last until the day she died.

Samantha

Another client, Samantha, was selling her house and relocating to a more expensive area. Her biggest concern was paying higher income taxes. She needed $270,000, and she was planning on taking a distribution from her investment account and IRA. My first piece of advice was to leave the money in her accounts and tap into her home equity in a way where she wouldn't be required to make a monthly payment. That strategy is known as a Home Equity Conversion Mortgage (HECM) for Purchase. More commonly, it's known as a reverse mortgage.

Reverse mortgages don't require a payment to be made to the mortgage company. There are a few different options when choosing a reverse mortgage, and each person's scenario is different so make sure you consult with a mortgage broker who specializes in reverse mortgages. I have a colleague who is a reverse mortgage specialist, and we work jointly with clients to come up with the best solution for them.

The HECM for Purchase is a loan that allows homeowners who are sixty-two years or older to purchase a new principal residence using loan proceeds from the reverse mortgage. It allows borrowers to purchase the home with a single down payment and does not require monthly payments. Homeowners must pay property taxes, homeowners insurance, and maintenance expenses to avoid foreclosure. Samantha didn't want to do that.

My next solution was for her to use her overfunded life insurance account that we had built up over the past six years, which she would back from another account that we had set up. She liked that idea. Remember, the overfunded life insurance is tax-free.

For the past six years, Samantha paid $60,000 a year in premiums with no additional premiums required. She also had an annuity with a guaranteed lifetime income of about $22,000. She took a net 0% cost loan against her life insurance policy, paid back $130,000 as soon as she sold the old house, and used the $22,000 from her annuity to pay back the loan. She was able to get a net 0% interest loan because the loan was 3%, but at the same time, the cash value was credited 3% effectively giving her a net 0% cost loan. Her tax situation remained exactly the same even though she took out $270,000!

Besides the tax benefit, she also got a better price on the house because it was an all-cash deal. She didn't have to withdraw funds from her investment accounts and miss any potential gains in the market. Had she not worked with me, she would have been stuck paying capital gains tax (yes, her account is up in this down market) and income tax on the amount she withdrew. If she withdrew it all from the IRA, she would move up to the 35% tax bracket and would have had to pay an additional $94,500 in taxes. Her social security was already being taxed at the highest level, and her Medicare Part B premiums would have increased because of her higher income. I was able to help her accomplish all of her goals in the most tax efficient way.

Another benefit of this great policy is that she can use it for long term care costs if she cannot perform two out of the following six activities of daily living: (i) bathing, (ii) dressing, (iii) eating, (iv) transferring, (v) toileting, and (vi) continence. Let's not forget the $1,000,000 death benefit.

All of her friends wanted to be in this type of financial position. Who wouldn't? That is why I stress the importance of working with, ideally, a CFP® or another financial professional. When people try to handle their finances on their own, they miss out on strategies like these because they simply are not aware of them or how to use them effectively.

Pam

Pam came to me a few years ago, needing to withdraw $10,000 from her IRA. She was under age 59 ½, so on top of income taxes, she would also have a 10% early distribution penalty. I was able to reduce her penalty and taxes by withdrawing the money from an over-funded life insurance account we had set up.

When I first took Pam on as a client, she was frustrated that her IRA account hadn't grown in twenty years. She had been with several different advisors at this point. The account was small, and she wasn't continually funding it. I explained that even if she earned 20% in one year, that wasn't a large return because her account would remain small if she relied solely on market gains to increase its value without also making annual contributions.

Long- term market returns are about 8%. Since she was a conservative investor, I suggested she use another strategy to help her save for and supplement her retirement. She put paid $150 a month into the overfunded life insurance policy and $416.66 a month into her IRA. At the time, $5000 was the maximum you could contribute to an IRA. She wasn't thrilled about paying for life insurance until the day she called me and needed $10,000. I explained to her that this is why we did this so we wouldn't have to tap into her IRA in the event of an emergency. Life is unexpected and emergencies do happen. In that moment, she realized why the life insurance was an important part of her overall financial plan.

Conclusion

I hope you found this book enjoyable and informative. My goal was to inspire you and give you practical advice to assist you in reaching your financial goals. If you like what you read and want help on your particular situation feel free to reach out to me at: www.dsfinancialstrategies.com

If you wish to hire me as a speaker for your event, please contact me at (215)660-0288 or email Dawn@dsfinancialstrategies.com.

I wish you continued success on your journey. I would love to hear your experiences of how the prayer in this book worked for you. Remember your prayer will always be answered just not always in the way you think it should. "...Or something better."

About the Author

Dawn Santoriello, CFP® is the founder and CEO of DS Financial Strategies, a fee-based financial planning firm that develops customized plans designed to maximize the efficiency of your money.

Born in Brooklyn, NY and raised in Long Island, Dawn graduated from Adelphi University with a BS in Finance. She currently lives in King of Prussia, PA. Away from the office, you can find Dawn living true to her Wellness and Wealth lifestyle by hiking, kayaking, mountain biking, and meditating.

Dawn was the former host of *Conquer Your Finances, Conquer Your Life* on RVN TV. She has been published in numerous blogs and journals, including *Wealth Planning Advisor* and *Let's Talk Philadelphia* and has been featured in *Forbes*, *Investment Advisor*, *Market Watch*, and *The Philadelphia Inquirer*.

Be sure to check out Dawn's YouTube page (DS Financial Strategies) for "Financial Friday's with Dawn." For more information or to get in touch with Dawn, please visit:
www.dsfinancialstrategies.com

Photo courtesy of Marikate Venuto

Bibliography

Anonymous. "Confessions of a Former Mutual Funds Reporter." *CNN Money*, 2020.
https://money.cnn.com/magazines/fortune/fortune_archive/1999/04/26/258745/index.htmOriginally published in *FORTUNE Magazine*, 26 April 1999.

Bessembinder, Hendrik (Hank), Do Stocks Outperform Treasury Bills? (May 28, 2018). Journal of Financial Economics (JFE), Forthcoming, Available at SSRN: https://ssrn.com/abstract=2900447 or http://dx.doi.org/10.2139/ssrn.2900447

Bicycle Helmet Safety Institute. (2017). *Statistics from New York City.* https://helmets.org/stats.htm

Darlin, D. (2017, January 4). *It's Time to Ignore Advice About Which Stocks to Buy in 2017*. The New York Times. https://www.nytimes.com/2017/01/04/upshot/its-time-to-ignore-advice-about-which-stocks-to-buy-in-2017.html

Kinniry, F.M., Jr, et al.. (2019). *Putting a value on your value: Quantifying Advisor's Alpha*. Vanguard. https://advisors.vanguard.com/iwe/pdf/ISGQVAA.pdf

Ohio National Financial Services. (2020). *Life Insurance Retirement Supplement: Manage your retirement income with life insurance* [Brochure]. Ohio National Financial Services, Inc.

Rosenberg, A. (2015, August 31). *The inspiring story of the worst market timer ever*. CNBC.

https://www.cnbc.com/2015/08/27/the-inspiring-story-of-the-worst-market-timer-ever.html

Time, Not Timing, Is What Matters. (2020). Capital Group. https://www.capitalgroup.com/individual/planning/investing-fundamentals/time-not-timing-is-what-matters.html#:%7E:text=Rather%20than%20trying%20to%20predict,the%20timing%20of%20your%20investments.

Unlock Your "Money Blocks" How Women Can Break Through These 5 Barriers to Experience Financial Empowerment. (2020). [E-book]. Snappy Kraken. https://financeinsights.net/VmDC0DeuGwkB